"Diary of a Conscious Believer"

A Written Journey

(By Faraji Toure')

Diary of a Conscious Believer

Copyright © March 1, 2016, By Faraji Toure'

SquareBiz, LLC

ISBN: 978-0692834619

Preface

This book, *the diary of a conscious believer*, is a short collection of essays, completed works, thoughts and questions centered on religion and spirituality that I labeled my spiritual diary.

I decided to write and publish this book, and those to come, to inspire those who read it to question and then challenge the religious status quo. I hope to provoke you to begin your spiritual journey towards your ultimate truth about who God is and who you are in the "greater all."

It's my opinion that organized religion is *killing God*. So, I urge those among us who believe in God to read and study the bible, Qur'an, Torah or whichever Holy book you chose, in its entirety and question everything it. I urge you to read every "Holy" book you can find, including those on religious history. Most importantly pray, meditate and seek God internally.

Fighting over religious beliefs and ceremonies takes away from what God intended for us, it takes away from the truth and leaves us vulnerable to be manipulated and controlled. By finding answers for ourselves, we get closer to understanding our power and purpose.

God gave us laws and commandments to follow; he did not give us religion.

Dedication

I dedicate this book to both my parents T'Chaka M. Al-Moravids and Dr. Gloria J. East – Henderson, whom together has planted the seed of Spirituality in me.

Thank you for teaching me the differences between Spirituality, Faith and Religion.

Thank you

I sincerely want to thank God for putting the unshakable seed of the book in my spirit for me to birth, and for giving me the divine purpose of standing in the gap to usher people from spiritual ignorance into their ultimate truth.

Table of Contents

At War with Ourselves

Growing up in the church, I naturally became friends with people who were members of other churches. I remember witnessing people make fun of different denominations, to the point where neighbors got into arguments over parking spaces. During these exchanges, the faith they belonged to is mentioned, coupled with some unkind words.

I believe doctrine is accepting a person's interpretation of the bible, and that makes a denomination different. However, is it worth fighting and backbiting? I thought that the text taught patience, tolerance, peace, and acceptance. If I'm wrong about that, then someone, please help me to understand why isn't perseverance, understanding, friendship, and acceptance granted to those who don't worship as we do? This can also apply to other religious systems as well. Not every church is going to believe that you get into heaven by rolling around on the church floor and speaking in tongues; just like church women wearing oversized bright colored hats doesn't make them any more dignified than anyone else.

I can remember feeling like I needed to be in the presence of God while traveling and recalled seeing a church on my daily routes going to get food. I stopped in on a whim to pray, and I was wearing a collared shirt, blazer, jeans, and hard bottom shoes. Before I could get in the church good, I was approached and asked why did I come in the church dressed the way I was. At that moment, the deacon stated that if I can dress up to go to the club or out on a date, then I could dress up for Yeshua (Jesus). The deacon jokingly stated that I must be from a non-denomination church because a "Baptist" would know better. I began to feel so wrong about showing up without a suit that I didn't attend service that day.

I thought to myself, what if I was God or an angel sent by God to bless some people there, or usher people to heaven before the rapture and I get turned away like that? I know there is nowhere in the bible that says "come as you are," but I'm also sure it doesn't mean I must be in a three-piece suit either. I guess to their benefit; the Most-High didn't send me because they surely would have missed out. So why was I turned away again? Oh, that's right, because God requires a suit and tie to attend a gathering of churchgoers.

Matthew 11:28
Come to me, all who labor and are heavy laden, and I will give you rest
Isaiah 55:1
Come, everyone who thirsts, come to the waters; and he who has no money, come, buy and eat! Come; buy wine and milk without money and without price.

James 4:8

Draw near to God, and he will draw near to you. Cleanse your hands, you sinners, and purify your hearts, you double-minded.
Matthew 16:24
Then Jesus told his disciples, "If anyone would come after me, let him deny himself and take up his cross and follow me.
Revelation 22:17
The Spirit and the Bride say, "Come." And let the one who hears say, "Come." And let the one who is thirsty come; let the one who desires take the water of life without price.

As you can see, there is nothing in those scriptures, or any other scripture in the bible that I could find, that says anything about being dressed up, so your outer appearance is appealing to God.

To my knowledge and understanding, every holy book has an underlying theme across them all; take care of your fellow man, do good to others, and do unto others as you would have others do unto you. That's it, no more, no less real. Of course, there are examples in the form of stories and the Ten Commandments that help you obtain that simple premise. And the world would be in a better state, in my opinion, if this were to take place. You would also need everyone to desire peace, and we all know that there are people with wickedness and destruction in their hearts.

Let's not lie; poking fun at others for one reason or another can warrant a chuckle or even a good laugh at times. Even in my unenlightened stage, I got a good laugh from some of the antics, but on a deeper level, it's not funny because it's just one more layer of garbage that keeps people from unifying.

Denominations and labels are another divisive energy that keeps everyone at war and unfocused. No real change or healing can take place when we focus on menial things like who knows the right way to worship or the right way to get into heaven. My thought is if we are not following the laws set in the bible, but instead, following doctrine, we are in error.

The church can't even agree on how to get to heaven.

Some believe you cannot enter heaven unless you're baptized, others think you can't enter heaven unless you speak in tongues. Not only are believers at war with the outside world, but we are also at war with ourselves within the church body. Any system that attacks itself from within is a sickness.

The church body is sick.

I grew up in the church, a small "non-denominational" church on Bergen Street in Newark, New Jersey. Attending services here would be my earliest memory of church and

the place that would set the standard for any church I visited after that.

As a child, being dragged to church early Sunday mornings and not getting home until after 5 pm was sure to take a toll on my siblings and I. That didn't include the choir rehearsals, meetings, and church services during the week.

I can remember church members speaking about the differences between Baptist, Pentecostal, Catholic, and others. It never made much sense to me to say we belong to a non-denominational church, which is, in fact, a denomination. C.O.G.I.C or church of God in Christ is, in fact, a faith complete with its doctrine or way of viewing the laws in the Bible. I never understood why the churchgoers would turn their noses up or grimace in disgust if they were asked about another denomination or heaven forbid is mistaken for a member of another church.

I can remember thinking how much better off me, and other members of the church would be if we'd belong to another denomination. Judging from all the drama that took place in that small church, I just figured we shouldn't turn our noses up at people only because they didn't worship how we worshiped.

doc·trine

1.
A principle, position, or policy taught or advocated, as of a religion or Government: *Catholic doctrines; the Monroe Doctrine.*
2.
Something that is taught; teachings collectively: *religious d octrine.*
3. A body or system of teachings relating to a subject: *the doctrine of the Catholic Church.*

I made the connection with doctrine as an adult. In my search for a church home, I encountered many churches of the same supposed denomination, but with different and conflicting views.
Whether they are right or wrong is not relevant, and how I feel about them isn't either. I would hope that we, as believers in God, would get on the same page someday. Until that time, you would have to find the church that believes and worships in a way that you agree and makes you feel comfortable.

I had an engaging experience while visiting a church with a friend. After the sermon, the pastor asked if there is anyone who wants prayer or wants to join the church. Well, I guess the pastor had it out for me because he pretty much made a big deal about me joining the church right there on the spot. He went on to tell me that my future wife was there at the church, and I would go on to do great things under his guidance and leadership, none of which I believed for a single minute. Under feeling an extreme amount of pressure, I joined the church, and after I'd taken my seat, the pastor begins to speak about what the church believes. He spoke out against women wearing pants, make-up, and large earrings or playing billiards or card games because they were of the devil. He also went on to inform me that I must seek his guidance and approval with any significant decision in my life from that point forward. I never returned to his church after that day. I felt it was a church waist-deep in witchcraft to make such a demand that I turn over decisions of my life to a man I've just met because he is a pastor of the church.

False images

As the world begins to awaken to the reality that the images we tend to worship as God and Jesus are practicing idolatry, I'd be remiss not to speak on this topic.

First, let me state that my understanding of why worshipping idols isn't a good thing is that it causes you to think "outwardly" instead of "inward." We've seen the image of God and Jesus plastered in bibles, on that backside of church fans, tambourines, and church literature since I can remember, at least in the black churches. As far as I can remember, God and Jesus are depicted as some blond-haired blue eye Caucasian man. We now know this is by design.

Additionally, we know now that the world-famous picture of "Jesus Christ" is the image of Leonardo da Vinci's boyfriend, Cesare Borgia. And similarly, I'll give you a quick break down on whom the Catholic Church chose to represent their image of Jesus, the messiah. And as you can guess at this point, I am urging you, the reader, to do your research on the council of Nicea. *The committee that was held at Nicea in Bithynia* to get a proper back history on why these meetings were so crucial to Christianity.

Cesare Borgia, in the years between 1502 and 1503, employed the famous painter Leonardo da Vinci as an architect and engineer for one reason or another. And at some point, the two men became lovers, yes Cesare Borgia and Leonardo de Vinci. And because this was a time before cameras, camera phones and the endless apps we use to take pictures, Leonardo painted many images of his lover Cesare. Cesare's father, Rodrigo Borgia, had become Pope Alexander the fourth and under the authority of the Catholic Church gave his sons picture to be used as the image of Jesus Christ to trick the world into thinking Christ was European ultimately.

Two more notable things about this Cesare Borgia character; I'm not sure if the entire family practiced incest or if it was just him, but he had sex with his sister Lucrezia. He also killed his brother Giovanni Borgia in 1497. That doesn't sound like anyone worthy of being the image of Christ to me. For this and so many other reasons, I won't go into here.

I have an issue with honoring anyone other than God, and I'll tell you why. I came across *Isaiah 42:8*, as a young child and question my mother about it. My mother's explanation was that God and Jesus were the same person so forget about it.

Isaiah 42:8

"I am the LORD; that is my name! I will not give my glory to anyone else, nor share my praise with carved idols.

My next question is, does the 'cross' qualify as a graven image? Some have the little man that represents Jesus Christ, and others do not. We've already pointed out in the bible where the cross may be an Asherah Pole. We looked at scripture stated that they should be broken and or burned.

Leviticus 26:1

"Do not make idols or set up carved images, or sacred pillars, or sculptured stones in your land so you may worship them. I am the LORD your God.

It's my opinion that to serve our spirits better, we need to focus inward. Believers need to tap into the inner power of who we are and our abilities. Looking outward causes us to depend on others and view outside sources as our saviors, then we always look for someone else to save us. Furthermore, it causes us not to be responsible for our healing, happiness, or anything else. It allows us to pass the spiritual buck and blame God's will for things in our lives working out or not working out.

How often have you said, well, it must not have been in God's plan for me? Just think about every time you've heard or said that how much energy or an effort had you put into that one thing? If you're honest with yourself, you'd see that it's highly likely that you didn't put much energy into getting what you wanted.

It's also my belief and Over-standing that we can connect to God without a middle man. No deacon, reverend, bishop, pastor, or church member has any greater Understanding of our need than we who can go to God directly to get answers.

Given the fact that there are numerous scriptures in the bible that you shouldn't make or worship idols, I'm just dealing with the aspect of a "bigger" picture beside the passages that state the reason because God is jealous. I just refused to accept that God can be insecure. What could the omnipotent God possibly be jealous of? Who would attribute such a 'Human' emotion to God?

Exodus 20:4-6
"You must not make for yourself an idol of any kind or an image of anything in the heavens or on the earth or in the sea. You must not bow down to them or worship them, for I, the Lord your God, am a jealous God who will not tolerate your affection for any other gods. I lay the sins of the parents upon their children; the entire family is affected—even children in the third and fourth generations of those who reject me. But I lavish unfailing love for a thousand generations on those who love me and obey my commands.

Deuteronomy 4:23-24
Be careful not to forget the covenant of the LORD your God that he made with you; do not make for yourselves an idol in the form of anything the LORD your God has forbidden. For the LORD your God is a consuming fire, a jealous God.

Exodus 34:14
Do not worship any other god, for the LORD, whose name is Jealous, is a jealous God.

Colossians 3:5
Therefore, consider the members of your earthly body as dead to immorality, impurity, passion, evil desire, and greed, which amounts to idolatry.

Deuteronomy 4:16-18
So, that you do not act corruptly and make a graven image for yourselves in the form of any figure, the likeness of male or female, the likeness of any animal that is on the earth, the likeness of any winged bird that flies in the sky, the likeness of anything that creeps on the ground, the likeness of any fish that is in the water below the earth.

Psalm 97:7
All who worship images are put to shame, those who boast in idols– worship him, all you gods!

The Bunny Deception

When Easter is upon us, the masses go out buying new clothes, getting their hair and nails done, and are making plans to visit a church most haven't visited all year, if ever.

I know that many of us have, even if passively, thought about the meaning of Easter. The holiday marks the resurrection of Jesus of Nazareth, who was crucified and rose again on the third day. When the disciples went to retrieve Jesus' body, they've come to find that his body was no longer at its resting place.

Given what we know of this telling in the bible, my question is at this point, like so many others before me, I ask, where the hell did the Easter bunny come in to play? I have nothing against coloring eggs, hunting for eggs, dressing up, or visiting a church for that matter. But I pose a legitimate question; how did the world go from acknowledging the resurrection of Christ, to the more widely publicized Easter bunny? I can't see the connection between the two icons. And my follow up question is, why would a shift in focus even take place?

It appears not many people even care about such a shift in consciousness. Many see this holiday as a day they can spend money on new outfits and dress up and go to church for their once a year blessing. And to note Easter falls on the first Sunday, which is a day most churches conduct the communion ceremony. What's the big deal you ask? Well, during the service, the bible verse **1 Corinthians 11:26-28** is read:

1 Corinthians 11:26-28
26 "for whenever you eat this bread and drink this cup; you proclaim the Lord's death until he comes. 27 Therefore, whoever eats the bread or drinks the cup of the Lord in an unworthy manner will be guilty of sinning against the body and blood of the Lord. 28 A man ought to examine himself before he eats of the bread and drinks of the cup."

How many of us pay attention to that scripture? Service is so long on this day that by the time they finish passing around the juice and crackers, we are so hungry we want to eat and drink just to keep the service moving so we can get real food, not to mention looking good in our new outfits. But if you're visiting a church in the first place, I'm confident you have some type of belief in the teaching of Christ. So in that state of mind, if we examined ourselves even to a minimal of standards, most of us would find that we are not worthy to take eat and drink of the body and blood of Christ; to "proclaim the lord's death until he comes."

my charge to all is, while you're sitting in the salons or barbershops, mall or your favorite retail spot buying arts and crafts for your children, think about the real reason for the day and try passing that knowledge on. Because this day is NOT about a bunny rabbit, or chocolate Easter eggs and dressing up, and at the core of what the day; it's not even about Christ.
If you are reading this, I will just assume that you go to church and have done some type of research regarding the religious ceremony. So as you know, the word Easter derives from the ancient name Ishtar, a pagan goddess and an

abomination to God. She is also known as Astarte in the historical literature and as Ashtoreth in the scriptures. The name "*Easter*" originated with the names of an ancient Goddess and God. Christian scholars stated that Easter named after Eostre (a.k.a. Eastre). Eostre was the Great Mother Goddess of the Saxon people in Northern Europe. Similarly, the "*Teutonic dawn goddess of fertility was known variously as Ostare, Ostara, Ostern, Eostra, Eostre, Eostur, Eastra, Eastur, Austron, and Ausos.*" Her name derived from the ancient word for spring: "eastre." There were similar Goddesses at the time known by other names in ancient cultures around the Mediterranean and celebrated in the springtime. Some of her other titles are

- Aphrodite, also called Cytherea and Cypris
- Ashtoreth from ancient Israel
- Astarte from ancient Greece
- Demeter from Mycenae
- Hathor from ancient Egypt
- Ishtar from Assyria
- Kali, from India
- Ostara a Norse Goddess of fertility
- Semiramis

So just like everything else that has variations and multiple names, forms, and locations, this will get very confusing. I can't keep it all straight, so please, I implore you to do your research. Ishtar was an ancient Mesopotamian goddess of war, fertility, and sex. Those who worshiped her were involved in animal sacrifices and temple prostitution. Easter was originally the celebration of Ishtar, the Assyrian and

Babylonian goddess of fertility and sex. Her symbols are the egg and the bunny and still are fertility and sex symbols. After Constantine decided to convert the empire to Christianity, Easter was changed to represent Jesus. But at its roots, Easter is all about celebrating fertility and sex," which coincides with springtime, new beginnings, the new year. Not about any resurrection from the dead in a literal sense.

The images of Ashtoreth were of a large bare-breasted woman holding a rabbit in one hand and an egg in the other. As sexy as that may sound to some of us, it was not pleasing to God. God did not want his people to have anything to do with the custom and practices of worshiping pagan images or, more especially follow Ashtoreth or any other God.

In **Samuel 7:3-4**, Samuel tells Israel not to continue to worship other Gods and turn their hearts to God so they can be delivered from the Philistines.

Samuel 7:3-4

And Samuel spake unto all the house of Israel, saying, if ye do return unto the LORD with all your hearts, then put away the strange gods and <u>Ashtaroth</u> from among you, and prepare your hearts unto the LORD, and serve him only: and he will deliver you out of the hand of the Philistines. Then the children of Israel did put away <u>Baalim</u> and <u>Ashtaroth</u>, and served the LORD only.

So to my surprise, I found that the very wise King Solomon, in his old age, has once again made a not so smart decision while reading **1 kings 11:4-6**. King Solomon began to follow behind Ashtoreth, for some reason, and God was not pleased about it.

1 Kings 11:4-6

As Solomon grew old, his wives turned his heart after other gods, and his heart was not fully devoted to the LORD his God, as the heart of David his father had been. ⁵ He followed Ashtoreth the goddess of the Sidonians, and Molek the detestable god of the Ammonites. ⁶ So Solomon did evil in the eyes of the LORD; he did not follow the LORD completely, as David his father had done.

Several examples throughout the Bible shared the sentiment that Ashtoreth was not to be worshipped. The Bible refers to the Asherah poles as well. And to refresh your memory, an Asherah pole is a sacred tree or pole that stood near-religious locations to honor the mother-goddess Asherah, often referred to in the Bible as the "Queen of heaven." To make a quick mention that some religious scholars feel that the sign of the cross is considered an Asherah pole marking a holy site.

Biblically, one of the reasons Israel divided was due to their worship of Ashtoreth and other Pagan Gods.
God got fed up and decided to split the nations.

1 Kings 11:33

I will do this because they have forsaken me and worshiped Ashtoreth the goddess of the Sidonians, Chemosh the god of the Moabites, and Molek the god of the Ammonites, and have not walked in obedience to me, nor done what is right

in my eyes, nor kept my decrees and laws as David,
Solomon's father, did.

As usual, once God's wrath is incurred, there is a unified change of heart by the masses. We see this example over and over in the bible.

God or one of the prophets inform the people of what is required. People then do what the hell they want, then cry to avoid or stop the repercussions of being judged by God.

I'm sure this sounds familiar, and I'm 100 percent sure that you, the reader, have done this just as I have. In **1 Samuel 12:10**, they were no different, crying out to God to deliver them from their enemies so they can then worship him like he asks the first time.

1 Samuel 12:10
And they cried unto the LORD, and said, We have sinned,
because we have forsaken the LORD, and have served
Baalim and Ashtaroth: but now deliver us out of the hand
of our enemies, and we will serve thee.

Judges 10:6-7
6 And the children of Israel did evil again in the sight of the LORD, and served Baalim, and Ashtaroth, and the gods of Syria, and the gods of Zidon, and the gods of Moab, and the gods of the children of Ammon, and the gods of the Philistines, and forsook the LORD, and served not him.

7 And the anger of the LORD was hot against Israel, and he sold them into the hands of the Philistines, and into the hands of the children of Ammon

The (very short) Story of Semiramis

Semiramis was the wife of Nimrod and the mother of Tammuz (confusing, I know). After many years Semiramis died. She was also known as the "mother of god(s)" [you should research why] and had so much favor with the Gods they sent her back to earth as the spring fertility Goddess.

As I mentioned before, she is depicted as an exaggeratedly endowed bare-chested woman, often a queen, with crown, and an object of sexual desire. So the "Queen of Heaven" was basically "born again" as the Goddess Easter (Ashtarte – Ashtoreth, you get the point).

She popped out of a giant egg that landed on the Euphrates river sometime around sunrise on the Sunday after the vernal equinox. To claim her divine powers, she changed a bird into an egg-laying rabbit.
As her following grew, the high priest of Easter would impregnate young virgins on the altar of the fertility Goddess and sunrise on Easter Sunday. A year later, these same priests, or others, would then sacrifice those same babies on the alter and dye eggs in the blood of the dead babies.

This is just a short version of the story, but in any case, you can get a glimpse as to why God doesn't want anyone worshiping Ashtoreth. As a reminder, several scriptures instruct believers not to follow Ashtoreth but to destroy all the places marked with an Asherah pole.

Deuteronomy 12:1-4

These are the statutes and judgments, which ye shall observe to do in the land, which the LORD God of thy fathers giveth thee to possess it, all the days that ye live upon the earth.
Ye shall utterly destroy all the places, wherein the nations which ye shall possess served their gods, upon the high mountains, and upon the hills, and under every green tree:
And ye shall overthrow their altars, and break their pillars, and burn their groves with fire; and ye shall hew down the graven images of their gods, and destroy the names of them out of that place.
Ye shall not do so unto the LORD your God.

Deuteronomy 12:31, 32

Thou shalt not do so unto the LORD thy God: for every abomination to the LORD, which he hateth, have they done unto their gods; for even their sons and their daughters they have burnt in the fire to their gods.
What thing so ever I command you, observe to do it: thou shalt not add thereto, nor diminish from

Good Friday

The sad thing about all this is that today's believers who think they are honoring Christ on this day are honoring the day of the fish God Dagan, which is Friday. And yes, I know some of you are scratching your head at this point. As a point of reference, let me remind you that to find information on some of the things mention here, you must remember that Constantine mixed the Hebrew faith with pagan Gods, ceremony and rituals, and you must dig in mythology and religious history.

Christians will tell you that Christ changed the meaning of Good Friday, but there is no proof in the bible to prove that. Furthermore, Christians will tell you they are mimicking Jesus by fasting for 40 days, but what they are mimicking is the time and way the pagans wept for forty days for Tammuz, the sun god. Those believers that worshipped the son of Nimrod, the sun God, set aside forty days of mourning for Tammuz. These same believers honored "Lent" one day of each year of his incarnation, in which they would deny themselves a worldly pleasure for his pleasure in the afterworld.

Ezekiel 8

And it came to pass in the sixth year, in the sixth month, in the fifth day of the month, as I sat in mine house, and the elders of Judah sat before me, that the hand of the Lord GOD fell there upon me.

² Then I beheld, and lo a likeness as the appearance of fire: from the appearance of his loins even downward, fire; and from his loins even upward, as the appearance of brightness, as the colour of amber.

³ And he put forth the form of a hand, and took me by a lock of mine head; and the spirit lifted me up between the earth and the heaven, and brought me in the visions of God to Jerusalem, to the door of the inner gate that looketh toward the north; where was the seat of the image of jealousy, which provoketh to jealousy.

⁴ And, behold, the glory of the God of Israel was there, according to the vision that I saw in the plain.

⁵ Then said he unto me, Son of man, lift up thine eyes now the way toward the north. So I lifted up mine eyes the way toward the north, and behold northward at the gate of the altar this image of jealousy in the entry.

⁶ He said furthermore unto me, Son of man, seest thou what they do? even the great abominations that the house of Israel committeth here, that I should go far off from my sanctuary? but turn thee yet again, and thou shalt see greater abominations.

⁷ And he brought me to the door of the court; and when I looked, behold a hole in the wall.

⁸ Then said he unto me, Son of man, dig now in the wall: and when I had digged in the wall, behold a door.

⁹ And he said unto me, go in, and behold the wicked abominations that they do here.

¹⁰ So I went in and saw; and behold every form of creeping things, and abominable beasts, and all the idols of the house of Israel, portrayed upon the wall round about.

¹¹ And there stood before them seventy men of the ancients of the house of Israel, and in the midst of them stood Jaazaniah the son of Shaphan, with every man his censer in his hand; and a thick cloud of incense went up.

¹² Then said he unto me, Son of man, hast thou seen what the ancients of the house of Israel do in the dark, every man in the chambers of his imagery? for they say, the LORD seeth us not; the LORD hath forsaken the earth.

¹³ He said also unto me, turn thee yet again, and thou shalt see greater abominations that they do.

¹⁴ Then he brought me to the door of the gate of the LORD's house which was toward the north; and, behold, there sat women weeping for Tammuz.

¹⁵ Then said he unto me, Hast thou seen this, O son of man? turn thee yet again, and thou shalt see greater abominations than these.

¹⁶ And he brought me into the inner court of the LORD's house, and, behold, at the door of the temple of the LORD, between the porch and the altar, were about five and twenty men, with their backs toward the temple of the LORD, and their faces toward the east; and they worshipped the sun toward the east.

¹⁷ Then he said unto me, Hast thou seen this, O son of man? Is it a light thing to the house of Judah that they commit the abominations which they commit here? for they have filled the land with violence, and have returned to provoke me to anger: and, lo, they put the branch to their nose.

¹⁸ Therefore will I also deal in fury: mine eye shall not spare, neither will I have pity: and though they cry in mine ears with a loud voice, yet will I not hear them.

Since I explained the history of Nimrod/Tammuz elsewhere in this book all go into Dagan.

Dagan

Dagon was the head God of the Philistines, Dagon is said to be the father of Baal. He was the fish god and he was represented as a half-man, half-fish, (*dag* in Hebrew means "fish"). There are three places where Dagon is mentioned in the Bible. The first mention is *Judges 16:23*, where we are told that Dagon was the God of the Philistines. The Philistines offered "a great sacrifice" to Dagon, believing that their idol had delivered Samson into their hands. *1 Chronicles 10:10* mentions a temple of Dagon in which the head of King Saul was fastened. Then, in *1 Samuel 5*, Dagon was humiliated by the God of Israel.

1 Samuel 5:1-12

When the Philistines captured the ark of God, they brought it from Ebenezer to Ashdod. ² Then the Philistines took the ark of God and brought it into the house of Dagon and set it up beside Dagon. ³ And when the people of Ashdod rose early the next day, behold, Dagon had fallen face downward on the ground before the ark of the LORD. So they took Dagon and put him back in his place. ⁴ But when they rose early on the next morning, behold, Dagon had fallen face downward on the ground before the ark of the LORD, and the head of Dagon and both his hands were lying cut off on the threshold. Only the trunk of Dagon was left to him. ⁵ This is why the priests of Dagon and all who enter the house of Dagon do not tread on the threshold of Dagon in Ashdod to this day.

⁶ The hand of the LORD was heavy against the people of Ashdod, and he terrified and afflicted them with tumors, both Ashdod and its territory. ⁷ And when the men of Ashdod saw how things were, they said, "The ark of the God of Israel must not remain with us, for his hand is hard against us and against Dagon our god." ⁸ So they sent and gathered together all the lords of the Philistines and said, "What shall we do with the ark of the God of Israel?" They answered, "Let the ark of the God of Israel be brought around to Gath." So they brought the ark of the God of Israel there. ⁹ But after they had brought it around, the hand of the LORD was against the city, causing a very great panic, and he afflicted the men of the city, both young and old, so that tumors broke out on them. ¹⁰ So they sent the ark of God to Ekron. But as soon as the ark of God came to Ekron, the people of Ekron cried out, "They have brought around to us the ark of the God of Israel to kill us and our people." [11] *They sent therefore and gathered together all the lords of the Philistines and said, "Send away the ark of the God of Israel, and let it return to its own place, that it may not kill us and our people." For there was a deathly panic throughout the whole city. The hand of God was very heavy there.* [12] *The men who did not die were struck with tumors, and the cry of the city went up to heaven.*

In Conclusion, Christians celebrate Easter Sunday in honor of the resurrection of Jesus Christ, with the dying of Easter eggs, by eating ham and with a sunrise service all rooted in paganism. Every one of these rituals or ceremonies took from the pagan worship of the "Sun God." So why do we, as believers, ignore instructions for God in the scriptures?

What is your blessing tied to?

I went to visit my sister's church one Sunday, and she belongs to this grandiose church in the southern part of New Jersey. You know the type; big-screen televisions all over the place, sound and video department, an overfill room, the works. I've been to that church several times before but never became a member because the vibe wasn't right for me. I could never have my "God experience" there.

I would watch other churchgoers jump up and down and yell "preach" or "tell it rev," but I never quite got excited about what the pastor had to say, or nothing ever really hit home for me. And one Sunday, as I sat and listened to the pastor of that church speak offering time rolled around. And just like the Sundays I've visited previously, he would stand there and give the standard "offering speech" of **Luke 6:38** "Give, and it will be given to you. They will pour into your lap a good measure—pressed down, shaken together and running over. For by your standard of measure it will be measured to you in return."

He would finish this by saying something like "I don't need your money if you think I need your money then keep your money in your pocket" well, I did think he needed my money, so I did keep my money in my pocket. God doesn't need my money. But this big-screen TV, sound system, state of the art kitchen, books and CD's he was selling did need my money, and I wasn't for it, so yes, he did not get a single dime. Now don't get me wrong, in my unenlightened days, I did tithe monetarily, which I now know and feel to be incorrect.

Now on this day, that wasn't the only observation I made. As parishioners were marching to put their money in the tithe box, the pastor began to speak to the church.

Now I can't remember most of what he was talking about, but I remember very vividly that he stated to the church "y'all are bless, and you know the only reason you are blessed?" to which he and a host of churchgoers answered "because I'm blessed" I froze to make sure I heard that correctly, and yes he summarized right after by saying "that's right, y'all are blessed because I'm blessed, you can't go nowhere else and be blessed like this"

The room went silent as I went into my thinking to review that statement a few times internally to make sure I heard that statement in it's intended context. No matter how I chopped or diced it, that statement didn't sit well with me. To tell your followers that the only reason they are blessed is that they are under your guidance and leadership, how arrogant. I promptly removed myself from that church and never went back.

It's a shame that this behavior and mindset is commonplace; that being a spiritual leader is a hustle and not something a person is being "called" to do.

The verses in *Malachi 3:8-10* are the most misused in Scripture today. Every Sunday, pastors, deacons, reverends, and spiritual leaders use this verse to pry open the wallets of church members. It also says in verse 5 that the Most-High will judge them for it.

Malachi 3:8-10

8 Will a man rob God? Yet ye have robbed me. But ye say, wherein have we robbed thee? In tithes and offerings.
9 Ye are cursed with a curse: for ye have robbed me, even this whole nation.
10 Bring ye all the tithes into the storehouse, that there may be meat in mine house, and prove me now herewith, saith the Lord of hosts, if I will not open you the windows of heaven, and pour you out a blessing, that there shall not be room enough to receive it.

Malachi 3:5

5 And I will come near to you to judgment; and I will be a swift witness against the sorcerers, and against the adulterers, and against false swearers, and against those that oppress the hireling in his wages, the widow, and the fatherless, and that turn aside the stranger from his right, and fear not me, saith the Lord of hosts.

Chapter 3 of Malachi talks about the Levites and the other 11 tribes of Israel. It talks about fruits and meat that were to go to the Levites, who were the priest in charge of taking care of the Temples in Jerusalem and doing the sacrificial offerings. This is verified in **Deuteronomy 18: 1-5**. God does not need or want our money; He never has. The tithes were the first fruits, grains, and animals were to go to the Levites.

Deuteronomy 18: 1-5

The priests the Levites, and all the tribe of Levi, shall have no part or inheritance with Israel: they shall eat the offerings of the LORD made by fire, and his inheritance.
2 Therefore shall they have no inheritance among their brethren: the LORD is their inheritance, as he hath said unto them.
3 And this shall be the priest's due from the people, from them that offer a sacrifice, whether it be ox or sheep; and they shall give unto the priest the shoulder, and the two cheeks, and the maw.
4 The first fruit also of thy corn, of thy wine, and of thine oil, and the first of the fleece of thy sheep, shalt thou give him.
5 For the LORD thy God hath chosen him out of all thy tribes, to stand to minister in the name of the LORD, him and his sons forever.

Offerings were used as sin offering to the Most-High, and some to the Levites for food as it says in **Deuteronomy 18:1**.

One of the two laws Yeshua (Jesus) came to fulfill was the law of sacrifice. Yeshua offered Himself as the ultimate sacrifice, so we as believers no longer had to make sacrificial offerings. We no longer had to take our first fruits, grains, and meats to the Levites to sacrifice for us.

And if you're thinking that you should be paying the pastor to take care of the temple, or for pastoring, then, by all means, do what you feel is right. I can't tell you what to do with your money; I'm just informing you that it will be of your own free will to do so, and not a spiritual obligation.

Where did the belief come from that if you donated enormous amounts of money to a church; that guaranteed you a place in heaven? That's just as silly as saying a few Hail Mary prayers will absolve you from your sin. Please don't get me wrong, I do believe in redemption, but that goes hand in hand with repentance. I thought the point was not to sin at all and attempt to live the best life we can without harming others in following the laws of the Bible.

My belief is if you don't feel conflicted about your wrongdoings that only God knows, then paying money, confessing to a priest, or saying a few quick repetitive prayers won't do the trick either. I see it as the lazy man's approach to hoping they get into heaven. Am I correct when I say that the Bible says the wages of sin is death? To me, that means no afterlife, no heaven, and even no hell, just nothing you die, and you become a memory.

What close-minded sense of believing if we believe that God's love and favor are expressed only when good things happen to us, or our material possessions increased. I hear many pastors making statements like that. You mean to tell me that if I don't have a nice car, beautiful clothes, a good job, then God doesn't favor me? Or that I'm not blessed? Did not Jesus require men to leave their worldly possession behind and follow him? Who mentioned being in the world but not of it? You have read or heard these things spoken out of the Bible but allow yourselves to be fooled into believing that people have more of God's favor by the material possessions people amass. God is not concerned with the material properties of this world. Foolish kings and rulers have stuffed their most prized possessions in a casket with their corps only to have it later robbed by thieves.

I can imagine the wicked people who sit in church, even as you read this, planning to destroy another's life. I'm speaking of that one person who stays in every church activity that will smile and talk with sincere passion but has a heart as black as coal and ready to do wrong the first chance he or she gets. No amount of service to the church or money to the church will grant that person a happily ever after in heaven. I know that example is somewhat extreme, but think about it for a second, the idea is to change the adverse action or behavior to be in alignment with what the Most-High has set in place for peaceful and productive living.

The ills of Prosperity Preaching

Can anyone else remember when going to church meant saving your soul from eternal damnation? Being saved from the bottomless pit or the burning hellfire was the missing of spiritual leaders. Maybe even being tortured by Satan's imps and demons? Who knew that material money could set the soul on the straight and narrow path; I didn't.

I take issue with pastors around the world preaching nothing but prosperity. I believe that if you fix the soul, you fix the problems here on the physical plane. That last statement maybe a little naive, but I'm hopeful at times that the statement may be right. Every time I turn on the television, I see pastors talking about how to gain God's favor by sowing a financial seed, to them, of course. When in fact, there is nowhere in the bible or any holy book that states that to gain God's favor, you should give a pastor or church system your money. I thought it was by keeping Gods laws and commandments coupled with doing well to your fellow man that kept you covered in the Most-Highs good graces. Now unless the current version of the New Testament was once again "tweaked" to say so, I think my assessment is correct.

The only thing I've noticed about prosperity preachers is that they seem to have the system down pact in how to line their pockets with parishioner's money. They ask for 10 percent tithes, regular offering, speakers offering, anniversary offering, musicians offering, building fund, sick and shut-in offering, woman's day, men's day, youth choir, fix the bathroom offering and anything else they can think of to suck the money out of your pockets and into their tax-exempt bank accounts. And please don't think that saying you don't have cash is a sufficient excuse anymore, the usher will direct you to the nearest ATM in the building. If you have somehow survived all those pleas for money, after the service, they will be selling dinners, books, CD's and cassette tapes candy and t-shirts to make sure you're broke so you can keep coming to the church to receive your blessing.

I genuinely believe that *prosperity preaching* does more harm than good in our minority communities, and often our church leaders look just like us. Church leaders guilt-trip us into being "obedient" to them and not the word of God. Some of us are so lazy we won't open the Bible to read for ourselves what it says. But we will go around regurgitating what the pastor or deacon says like it's the law. The only thing the pastor in the pulpit is doing is keeping you out of alignment with what the Bible says is due to you if you were to seek God's face. That doesn't mean that you take the pastor's word for it; it means you do the work too.

You come to church week after week, barely enough money left over to feed you and your family and be fed lies, and your pocket sucked dry. The pastors are on their way to church with a joyful heart ready to collect their pay. They ride to church in style, dressed well, and will say, "look what God has done for me; I know the key to gain God's favor."

And you see that this person appears to be living better than you and you begin to idolize him or her. Now you need to know how to live better, too, so you follow and hang onto every word. You must remember that the word of God is given freely to every man, and you don't need to pay tuition to get that word, pick up a bible and begin to read, God will give you the over-standing you need to learn if you ask for it.

What about the Soul?

I subscribe to the idea that the world today is by design a distraction from our higher purpose of focusing on the Most-High (the inner self). We stay in a state of worry about bills, our careers, our loved ones, the world in general, and ourselves. We never have much time to sit and reflect or even pray. Sure, many of us attend church, mosque, or temple, but once that visit is done, we are back to worrying and stuck in a state of frustration and too confused to apply the method learned in our perspective houses of worship.

To add to that confusion, we must take into account that the information given is continuously watered down by the seemingly daily revising of the bible and its meanings and still seem not to understand what we are reading. Church figureheads, who seem to have a better understanding than most, seem to spoon-feed the church body spirituality wrapped in perverse notions that they should be honored, revered or worshipped. Operating this way is never meant for our good.

What happened to the church heads that wanted its members to get into heavens gates, the city with streets paved with gold? The land of milk and honey. These days you hear pastors giving out lessons on how to be a better participant in this world. We are taught how to unlock our blessings to get better homes, better clothes, and vehicles because God doesn't want us to struggle. We are seldom taught anything about forsaking this material world for the

Spiritual next, living the now for the promise of the infinite.

Job 14:1 states, *"Mortals, born of woman, are of few days and full of trouble."* And the goal was to pass from this life and hear the highest say *"well done thy good and faithful servant,"* and enter those pearly gates.

It's my understanding that we, as members of the twelve tribes of Israel, are in the predicament that we are currently in and subject to God's punishment because we turned away from our intended purpose, our calling, in the first place. We decided not to follow the laws given us, worshipped false idols and live perverse lifestyles and were punished because of it, disbanded and caused to be overtaken and enslaved. So why would God want us to have those material things we so quickly worship instead of him as blessings? Coveting material things is what got us here in the first place.

Tithing the Wrong Way?

The subject of tithing is a personal interest to me. Time and again, we see ourselves or fellow churchgoers giving their last bit of money to the church entrusting that God will bless them financially or grant his favor upon them for donating to the church.

I've witness pastors and deacons alike encouraging the congregation to donate more and more money even after the plate has passed around one or two times. I've also witnessed pastors give what I like to call a spiritual "guilt trip" to church members by quoting the bible verse from *Luke 6:38*

Luke 6:38

"Give and it will be given to you. A good measure, pressed down, shaken together and running over, will be poured into your lap. For with the measure you use, it will be measured to you."

The book of *Malachi 3:8-10* is used as well.

Malachi 3:8-10

"Will a man rob God? Yet ye have robbed me. But ye say, wherein have we robbed thee? In tithes and offerings".

I can also remember church leaders saying a "special" prayer over those who gave and alienating those church members who could not.

And of course, we are not tithing today the way church members did in the days when Yeshua (Jesus) walked the earth.

2 Chronicles 31:5
And as soon as the commandment came abroad, the children of Israel brought in abundance the first fruits of corn, wine, and oil, and honey, and of all the increase of the field; and the tithe of all [things] brought they in abundantly.

But I ask, why not? Why are we not bringing things like fruit, rice, non-perishables into the storehouse of the church? Would it not help those in the church community, that are in need?

2 Chronicles 31:10
"And Azariah the chief priest of the house of Zadok answered him, and said, Since [the people] began to bring the offerings into the house of the LORD, we have had enough to eat, and have left plenty: for the LORD hath blessed his people; and that which is left [is] this great store."

And since we can all agree that it's seldom for the institutional church to help a member in need, why are we tithing? Why not take up an additional "collection" to assist a member or family in need? What is the tithe used for?

Deuteronomy 26:12
When thou hast made an end of tithing all the tithes of thine increase the third year, [which is] the year of tithing, and hast given [it] unto the Levite, the stranger, the fatherless, and the widow, that they may eat within thy gates, and be filled

So now is tithing the way we attempt to buy our way into heaven? Or bribe God for his favor and grace? I hear time and time again; people are saying bad things happen when they don't tithe or better things happen when they do tithe, which I will say is a matter of personal belief, experience, and perspective.

And finally, God is not getting that money. And no one can successfully justify or explain how God is benefitting from me giving money to an institution that's not providing any service for me or my community that I can't obtain myself by picking up the bible and reading myself. And from the looks of things, the churches are getting bigger and bigger. So is the blessing of God on that church determined by how well that church is doing financially?

How does it say tithe in the bible?

As I stated earlier, I'm aware that the topic of tithing is a touchy one, especially for those that defend the current system of giving money to the church at all cost or you will not be blessed. As I stated before, God does not need a man-made system of currency trading for goods and services. And the first book of the bible I want to note in my explanation is Deuteronomy.

Deuteronomy 14:22-29 (ESV)

Tithes

[22] *"You shall tithe all the yield of your seed that comes from the field year by year.* [23] *And before the L*ORD *your God, in the place that he will choose, to make his name dwell there, you shall eat the tithe of your grain, of your wine, and of your oil, and the firstborn of your herd and flock, that you may learn to fear the L*ORD *your God always.* [24] *And if the way is too long for you, so that you are not able to carry the tithe, when the L*ORD *your God blesses you, because the place is too far from you, which the L*ORD *your God chooses, to set his name there,* [25] *then you shall turn it into money and bind up the money in your hand and go to the place that the L*ORD *your God chooses* [26] *and spend the money for whatever you desire—oxen or sheep or wine or strong drink, whatever your appetite craves. And you*

*shall eat there before the L*ORD *your God and rejoice, you and your household.* ²⁷ *And you shall not neglect the Levite who is within your towns, for he has no portion or inheritance with you.*

²⁸ *"At the end of every three years you shall bring out all the tithe of your produce in the same year and lay it up within your towns.*

²⁹ *And the Levite, because he has no portion or inheritance with you, and the sojourner, the fatherless, and the widow, who are within your towns, shall come and eat and be filled, that the L*ORD *your God may bless you in all the work of your hands that you do.*

It's clearly stated here how to tithe. So you forsaking yourself and family, to give only to the church/pastor, is nowhere in that scripture.

And what if you don't have money to tithe? Are you not blessed? We have already established that the church today is not tithing the way it was done in the days of Yeshua (Jesus). In those days, you were bringing a portion of your cattle or herd or anything that you grew or produced, like corn, flour, fruits, grains, and wine. No longer are those things acceptable as they cannot fit into the offering plate or the preacher's bank accounts.

I spoke with a friend recently, and she defended her church leaders by stating that the leaders in her church sell books, Recordings of their sermon and other things to build income instead of taking from the church body. If this is the case, then that's great, but I'm aware that not all figureheads are using this method.

Unfortunately, I have no examples from myself, friends or family members where a church stepped in to assist a person or family from their flock in the time of need outside of making an announcement to the church body and taking up a new collection for immediate relief to the problem. Even that example is better than my example of witnessing a woman pay tithe faithfully to the church for years. When she fell on hard times and brought it to the church's attention, she is told to "take it to the Lord in prayer," had a prayer said for her, and is ushered back to her seat among the congregation.

Some church leaders have full or part-time careers outside of the church. Some may also say that church leaders deserve some form of compensation for being the leader of a congregation. I can agree that there should be modest compensation. It seems as if the financial gap between church leaders and their group is getting broader. While the pastor shows up in expensive vehicles, their members are driving significantly cheaper cars, if they are driving at all.

But what if I don't have any money to give because I'm entirely destitute? What if I don't have an acceptable amount of money to give? Am I no longer covered under Gods' favor or not get into heaven?

Most churches preach prosperity and abundance in some form or fashion, but seemingly not for the average churchgoer. You are told your blessings are waiting in heaven, and it's received by faith and obedience to the pastor and church (not to God), but the churches and pastors blessing lie here on earth and within your wallet, and they will say anything to get their blessings.

It bothers me that people are profiting financially from repeating the word of God and the prophets that were given to the world freely.

Sixteen times in the bible, the tithe was mandatory by God to be only fruits, vegetables, and clean animals; never money, gold, silver, your wages, or anything else. And nowhere in the bible did God transfer tithe from the Levites to any apostle, prophet, evangelist, shepherd, pastor, bishop, teacher, church, religious organization, or anyone else.

Force Fed Religion

How soon we forget that, during the slavery era, we were force-fed this current religious system under the fear of being beaten, raped, or even killed. Has anyone stopped long enough to ask how is the same religion we are forced to believe in, is the same religion used to justify the reasons you kill me, discriminate against me and oppress me? Why am I taught to love my enemies and forgive my persecutors who say they worship the same deity as me? What type of person preaches that we should love their fellow man as you love yourself on the one hand and enslave and kill on the other?

We have become so brain washed we feel God will punish us for questioning the current state of the church. and that God will be displeased if we examine inconsistent "facts" that are laid out in our holy books, or question the motive, actions, and intentions of the so-called spiritual leaders. Essentially these church figure heads have not only become our over-seers, they have become another yoke upon us, another thumb pressed against the neck of the community. They keep a pulse on the temperament of the city and are deployed as watchdog mediators for the oppressors when temperatures run high to coax us back to sleep. They usher our frustrated energy into forward-moving non-actions like rallies and marches but never helping to usher in real change. Church leaders remind us to stay dormant and docile with quoted text and scripture while waiting for an external savior to make everything better.

The sad truth is that many of us have forgotten, or maybe refuse to believe that we should save ourselves. Our real strength will come once we realize that the power of change is in our hands. We are taught that not only do we need saving but that our help comes from somewhere or someone else.

For those of us that attend church, mosque, synagogue, or temple, it's essential to be consistent and offer up a prayer to whomever we worship and stay connected to the whole of our spirituality or religion if you so choose to do so. Often we are made to feel guilty for not going to our houses of worship, and some of us only attend because we feel obligated to, like it's something that we are just supposed to do. God not only exists inside of the church but live outside as well! *1 Corinthians 3:16-17* said it as well as *1 Corinthians 6:19-20*

1 Corinthians 3:16-17
Do you not know that you are God's temple and that God's Spirit dwells in you? If anyone destroys God's temple, God will destroy him. For God's temple is holy, and you are that temple.

1 Corinthians 6:19-20 (KJV)

¹⁹ What? Know ye not that your body is the temple of the Holy Ghost which is in you, which ye have of God, and ye are not your own?
²⁰ For ye are bought with a price: therefore, glorify God in your body, and in your spirit, which are God's.

in recent decades' information has become known about the tampering of the bible by ruling kings or popes of those times. and we still accept mediocre explanations on why. We take the teaching of the trinity, which does not exist biblically, and many other instructions we are told are factual that did not exist before it was agreed upon at the **Council of Nicea** in 325 AD, and it is not found in the bible. Nowhere in the scripture can you find Yeshua (Jesus) saying that he is God. I refer you to **John 8:39-41** as Yeshua (Jesus) responds to the Jews. There are countless other events concerning the bible being manipulated to fit a supremacy agenda. Still, believers find it difficult to break away from that yoke of ignorance and do the right thing.

John 8:39-41

39 They answered and said to Him, "Abraham is our father." Jesus said to them, "If you are Abraham's children, do the deeds of Abraham. 40 But as ut us, you are seeking to kill me, a man who has told you the truth, which I heard from God; this Abraham did not do.

41 "You are doing the deeds of your father." They said to Him, "We were not born of fornication; we have one Father: God."

Let's take the Sabbath as another example. The bible tells us in *Exodus 20:8-11* that the Sabbath is on Saturday. Most of us have read that for ourselves but still will not question why most of the world is going to church on a Sunday. Most believers refuse to even question such things even though we are charged with keeping it Holy.

After Rome adopted what we now call "Christianity", the Catholic Church changed the original doctrine of the Jews. A text quoted from the council of Laodicea, 363 A.D states "Christians must not Judaize by resting on the Sabbath, but must work on that day, rather than honoring the lord's day"

Exodus 20:8-11
Remember the Sabbath day, to keep it holy. Six days you shall labor and do all your work, but the seventh day is a Sabbath of the LORD your God; in it you shall not do any work, you or your son or your daughter, your male or your female servant or your cattle or your sojourner who stays with you. For in six days the LORD made the heavens and the earth, the sea and all that is in them, and rested on the seventh day; therefore, the LORD blessed the Sabbath day and made it holy.

Preaching Obedience with fear

As a child i recall kneeling at the foot of my mother's bed listening to stories from the bible. I can remember being terrified of the stories she told of the rapture when she would give us warning that one day we'd awaken or return from school and not be able to find her because she'd be "caught up" and taken to heaven. At the same time, my siblings and I will be left behind to fend for ourselves against Satan's demons and indescribable human-like monsters. Now, as a child whose security and mental peace depended on the connection between mother and child, with a vivid imagination, that was the most frightening thing to hear.

Our reality was that this account was told to us constantly, and put such a fear in me that if my mother was more than a few minutes last from work or church I would go into a panic. I would sit and wait for the sun to darken, the sky to turn blood red, a loud trumpet to sound and the demons and monsters to arrive to torture the world.

My mother used this fear of hell and the rapture she instilled in us to control my siblings and I. most of the rants ended with, "or you'll go to hell". She didn't abuse that power but to a child hearing this, everything got you sent to hell. Playing card games got you sent to hell, playing "worldly" music got you sent to hell, and of course the standard lying, cursing and fighting got you sent to hell as well. I never understood why my mother would tell a child such things until I was old enough to finally pay attention to the pastor of our small church in Newark, NJ and realized he was doing the same thing to the congregation. he would, every so often, tell a tale of a man walking into our church, and the man either cursed at the pastor or refused prayer, I can't recall which, but upon leaving the church he was hit by an automobile and decapitated. The pastor then ended that story as he always did with the phrase "touch not my anointed". The pastor used that term in a way that implied that he was above reproach. the pastor believed that if anyone questioned him or said anything against his words or actions that God would cut them down.

That mentality and attitude was a problem then as it is a problem in the church now. When researching the phrase "Do not touch My anointed ones, and do My prophets no harm.", exclusively used in the Old Testament, I found that the phrase was a reference for the kings of the nation of Israel. *(1Sam. 12:3,5; 24:6,10; 26:9,11, 16,23; 2 Sam. 1:14,16; 19:21; Psalm 20:6; Lam. 4:20)* and the mentioning of prophets represented the patriarchs *(Psalm 105:8-15; 1Chron. 16:15-22)*.

The word "touching" means to touch someone or cause them physical harm. The phrase does not mean that no one can say anything about another person, pastor, reverend, deacon or bishop. True, we should not bare false witness or slander anyone falsely, but we are allowed to speak the truth about someone.

God protected His anointed, who were the Kings of Israel, and the prophets from the enemies of Israel who sought to bring them physical harm. There are countless examples of people not touching Gods anointed, but speaking against God's anointed like David and Samuel spoke against Saul. Saul was anointed as King over Israel. he had a position of ruler-ship that was about to end. Knowing he was next in line David refused to physically touch the king and remove him from his position prematurely. It was God, not David who would remove Saul from his position. Even during King David's time in rule, he had accepted rebuke and correction from Nathan the prophet

I learned that spiritual leaders, including mine, would use this phrase to hide behind or invoke fear into anyone who would question their means or methods. It's the same response given when questioned why scare tactics are used to bring people into the church and to the alter to be saved. hearing premonitions and predictions, from the pastor, of when the world would end and most often no explanation of why it hadn't. I do remember one time hearing a short sermon about why God spared the earth. And that sermon came from the same man that would utter "no man knows the time or the hour of Jesus' return".

there was a pattern during every service where the organist would began playing this sad, melodramatic tune on the organ and the pastor's speech went from yelling loud to a low concerned tone. The pastor would start by shaking his head, wiping the sweat from his face and say "the world is waxing worse and worse". This course of events would put everyone in the frame of mind that he was concerned about where their soul went after death and he had the keys to get

you into heaven. This event was "alter call", where he was the saver of souls. He would point people out and say "God is speaking to me right now!" and point to people in the congregation and urged them to come up for prayer or to receive Christ as their lord and savior. I used to think this was an amazing thing and that he could hear God telling him about people's problems. That thought was dashed to pieces when I realized that the churches gossip network aided him in choosing who to call to the alter with vague mention of their problems.

Amongst all of this, people are being pointed out and told that they have sickness and the forces of darkness are in their homes or love ones and that they should come up for prayer. And of course, if you hear something like that you'd run to get prayer too.

One year my step father had death spoken over his life by the pastor of the church. After the pastor found out that my step father was unhappy with events going on at the church and began visiting another church more frequently, he was told, "If you leave this church you're going to die"

I feel that church leaders do this to keep up membership and aren't the least bit concerned with people's problems, situation or even their souls. Scaring people into coming to church is one way of keeping the church pews filled because Membership means dollars in the collection plate.

Profiting from the word

Prosperities

1.A successful, flourishing, or thriving condition, especially in financial respects; good fortune.
2. Prosperities, prosperous circumstances.

When speaking in terms of prosperity, the general thought is that any and every one can obtain prosperity. Today most sermons are filled with scriptures, quotes and examples about what needs to be done spiritually to align you with God's word to obtain financial prosperity. Give to God so God can give to you is the more common theory.

Being that we've already dealt with the fact that God doesn't need your "man-made" money to spread the word of God. he doesn't need monetary help to rebuild his kingdom here on earth, as I've heard it put before. Because those of us who read the bible know that your body is the dwelling place of God, the new temple.

1Corinthians 3:16-17
Do you not know that you are God's temple and that God's Spirit dwells in you? If anyone destroys God's temple, God will destroy him. For God's temple is holy, and you are that temple.

The question that arises now is, why are only the pastors prospering?

With the prosperity message being drilled in our heads as much as it is, why are our communities suffering?

I subscribe to the notion that you can lead a people to knowledge, but you can't make them think, as well as everyone is fully accountable to themselves. I came across several articles which stated that since the 80's black churches collected somewhere upwards of 420 billion dollars in tithes, offerings and donations.

In an article in the Atlanta Journal Constitution it notes that Reverend Creflo Dollar's World Changers Church reported taking in 69 Million Dollars in 2006. By any standard that's a nice piece of change to have come in during the year. My problem with that is, our community is being bled dry while being presented lengthy speeches about prosperity.

During one visit to Atlanta, I had the inclination to visit the World Changers' property. Upon arrival, I was greeted by a very large administration building that was far greater than most of the churches I've visited around the world. There were properties on both sides of the street, paid parking and a few other impressive things I noted. However, what struck me as odd was that the entire area surrounding the property was severally dilapidated. I couldn't piece together how an organization as big as this one could host so many outreach programs in other countries but forsake its own backyard. Not only are the people in the backyard being forsaken, the people in the church are being forsaken. It was publicized that boxer Evander Holyfield gave 10 percent of his 230 million dollars to the world changers ministry which came to about 23 million dollars then fell on hard times financially.

Do you think that Creflo Dollar and the World Changers ministry came to his aid? The answer again, no. To me this is not surprising at all. Mr. Dollar is the same "man of God" that stated non-tithers should be taken to the back of his church and shot as crooks for robbing God. He teaches that tithing is the connector between you and God.

Many church goers subscribe to the "Give God so God can give you" theory and will often reluctantly give their last dollar to the church. Yes, God love a cheerful giver and I'm sure these church leaders feel the same. How often does the giving (other than the word of God) goes the other way, from church to congregation? How many churches set up as communities within that help each other in time of need? I've seen some churches have classes on relationships, finances and health which are very much needed these days. Most of those classes are not free and if so still require an offering of sorts. Why does everything lead back to money? How many church leaders are sacrificing for the church? How many church leaders go without? The answer is, not many or none.

Some churchgoers will defend the idea that there financial blessing will come because they gave to the church by discounting the concern of what the pastor is doing with the money. After all, they gave from their heart. In the same notion, these same churchgoers will not give money to a homeless man for fear that he will squander it on drugs or alcohol not food. And as a reminder there is nowhere in the bible that states that God needs or wants your money, money will connect you to God or your giving money is the root cause of your blessings. Those are lies told to you by these prosperity preachers.

It would do better for you to help someone else in need with that money. You can feed a family, clothe a family and/or shelter a family with that money. You can use just your time and energy to ease the burden of someone else if you wanted to.

If your Religion needs money to survive, your God is fake!

1 John 4:1-6

Beloved, do not believe every spirit, but test the spirits to see whether they are from God, for many false prophets have gone out into the world. By this you know the Spirit of God: every spirit that confesses that Jesus Christ has come in the flesh is from God, and every spirit that does not confess Jesus is not from God. This is the spirit of the antichrist, which you heard was coming and now is in the world already. Little children, you are from God and have overcome them, for he who is in you is greater than he who is in the world. They are from the world; therefore, they speak from the world, and the world listens to them

What justifies profiting monetarily from the words given freely from God? If each one of us could get our hands on a holy book and read for ourselves the words given by God and passed down through the ages, it would put a major cramp in this machine called religion. May I remind you that the current church system is the same system that Yeshua (Jesus) rebelled against?

In *john 2:14-15* we saw that Yeshua (Jesus) made a whip out of rope and chased the business men out of the church. Our ignorance and brainwashing is lining these false prophets' pockets while they gladly lead their flock to slaughter.

John 2:14-16

14 And He found in the temple those who were selling oxen and sheep and doves, and the money changers seated at their tables. 15 And He made a scourge of cords, and drove them all out of the temple, with the sheep and the oxen; and He poured out the coins of the money changers and

Overturned their tables; *16 and to those who were selling the doves He said, "Take these things away; stop making My Father's house a place of business."*

Like many of you, I have personally witnessed these false prophets use and manipulate people for their gain, monetarily, for their sexual perversions, financial growth or whatever suits them best. The "Prophets" always conjure up some dream they had or vision God has supposedly given them about someone or something to impose their will. In my experience God, will always tell you what he needs to tell you and will send people or signs as confirmation. I'm always skeptical of people who begin their sentences with "God told me to tell you".

What's done or said out of love doesn't need promotion, if it's done with a genuine heart. Those who need to tell the world about the good deeds they've done is done with a heart full of ego and self-righteousness.

News cast are filled with stories of false prophets robbing church members of their money, fathering children out of wedlock, fathering multiple children with church members, adultery, pedophilia, and other perversions, the list goes on. How about the pastor that convinced the church that his penis had magic milk? He would take willing participants to his chambers and engage in oral sex until the "Holy Spirit" would release and enter their bodies. Even while incarcerated, the pastor stated that he will continue to "water his cellmates with his sacred milk".

Jeremiah 23:16

16. Thus says the LORD of host, "Do not listen to the words of the prophets who are prophesying to you. They are leading you into futility; they speak a vision of their own imagination, not from the mouth of the LORD. 17. "They keep saying to those who despise Me, 'The LORD has said, "You will have peace"; And as for everyone who walks in the stubbornness of his own heart, they say "Calamity will not come upon you"

We can turn on the news and see the state of the world getting progressively worse. However, our spiritual leadership rather addresses prosperity than encouraging it's members to become spiritually ready and aligned with their higher sense of self and purpose. We all love having nice things and places to stay, but a mansion on earth is still a

mansion in this hell hole. Money will not get you to heaven. Having nice cars, suits or any material thing made by the hands of man will not get you into heaven. So why aren't our spiritual leaders addressing these topics on a larger scale? All I hear is how God wants you to prosper and experience heaven while your here on earth.

John 14:1-2

1 "Man, who is born of woman, Is short-lived and full of turmoil. 2 "Like a flower he comes forth and withers. He also flees like a shadow and does not remain

Sowing a monetary seed of faith and reaping a financial harvest becomes the theme when it's time to give money. And church leaders also love to recite *2 Corinthians 9:6-8* and *Luke 6:38* during offering time.

I know I heard it on Sundays during service without pause. It amazes me how no one seems to feel that material sowing is sowing of the flesh, I undoubtedly know the Bible never made mention of sowing any financial seeds. Churches today take the scripture in theory and apply where needed. Furthermore, by reading *Galatians 6:7-10* we know that sowing in the flesh reaps corruption.

Galatians 6:7-10

Do not be deceived: God is not mocked, for whatever one sow, that will he also reap. For the one who sows to his own flesh will from the flesh reap corruption, but the one

who sows to the Spirit will from the Spirit reap eternal life. And let us not grow weary of doing good, for in due season we will reap, if we do not give up. So then, as we have opportunity, let us do good to everyone, and especially to those who are of the household of faith.

That passage states doing good, not giving good. God does not need your money...at all. Even if you're giving with a cheerful heart, God has no use for your money. Man, and his materialistic lust require your money. If you are catching the bus everywhere you need to go, or asking for rides because you need a vehicle, please save that 10% so you can purchase a vehicle. I'm sure your pastor is getting to church just fine. Better yet, your efforts would be better suited helping someone that may be in need instead of hoping the church would.

Why are you blessed?

The one thing I could never grasp is how some people feel that their blessings are tied to a church, profit or a pastor. I have witnessed some church leaders tell their congregation the reason they're blessed is because he/she, the pastor, is blessed. By all accounts we understand that the thought, words, idea or theory of that being remotely true is utter nonsense to the highest degree.

Is every man not worthy of receiving God's love and grace?

It's sad to say that often some church leaders attempt to set themselves up as a demigod to be worshipped and revered.

Some travel with an entourage complete with briefcase toting "armor bearers". You can always identify those members who fall for the demigod act because they will quote their pastor before they quote what's in the Bible. It's one thing to respect leadership, but to believe that your blessings come from them is insane. Where did this attitude come from? I don't recall reading anywhere in the Bible where Yeshua (Jesus) is requiring special treatment. Somewhere between then and now this self-righteous attitude has over taken these supposed "righteous" men of God.

Isaiah 42:8

I am Yahweh, which is my name; I will not give my glory to another or my praise to idols.

Nowhere in the Bible does it state or imply that church leaders are the reason their congregations are blessed. Every man and woman are not only accountable for themselves, but able to receive God's blessing for themselves, not just in the presence of the pastor or because they are covered as a member of their church. I also reject the act of a pastor "laying hands" on people. I used to ask myself who gave this person special powers to heal people? Is he much closer to God than I that he has power to heal? How could the same man who couldn't heal himself from a common cold to make it to church, heal someone else. Then I came across a verse in the bible **James 5:14-16**

James 5:14-16

Is anyone among you sick? Let him call for the elders of the church, and let them pray over him, anointing him with oil in the name of the Lord. And the prayer of faith will save the one who is sick, and the Lord will raise him up. And if he has committed sins, he will be forgiven. Therefore, confess your sins to one another and pray for one another, that you may be healed. The prayer of a righteous person has great power as it is working.

After reading that in the Bible, I would go to get prayed over time and time again and seldom felt any different once it over. Often my neck got a good workout as the preacher would rotate my neck so far back to throw me off balance amidst all the screaming while praying the preacher was doing. And on a few occasions, I remember being caught up in the wave of emotions of the church. People praising, screaming, crying falling out and rolling around on the floor of the church caused me to get caught up and I shed a few tears as well. Other times I found myself emotional due to gratitude over a blessing or circumstances, however there were times when I may have been hurting inside and to hear someone identify with that pain caused me to shed more than a few tears.

I never knew how one could make the mistake of attributing what God has done for what the pastor has tried to take credit for. The gross misrepresentation of the Bible easily passes because most church goers don't read the bible for themselves. Even those who attempt to are confused by verbiage used in it. And there is a new, translation published every week which only turns out to be a watered-down version of the translation. What good does that do for anyone?

These present church leaders are following the tradition of our absent overseers by keeping us confused and off track to receive spiritual health. They have scared us to the point where we don't demand accountability or minimally get answers other than "lean not into your own understanding" which is quoted from **Proverbs 3:5-6**

Proverbs 3:5-6
*Trust in the L*ORD *with all your heart and lean not on your own understanding;*
⁶ in all your ways submit to him, and he will make your paths straight

That passage doesn't say trust in your preacher, pastor, deacon or reverend and allow them to keep you spiritually ignorant. The solution to this problem doesn't just rest on the shoulders of these church leaders. The responsibility falls on the church community as well. To hold the individual accountable for the things they teach and the lies they tell. It starts with knowing God for yourselves. Pick up a bible and read, ask questions until you are satisfied. If your church leader refuses to answer questions or don't know the answer, go ask another pastor, read another book until the answer sits true in your spirit.

These pastors may not be righteous enough to bless us, but we can also assess by what the church leaders of today are teaching and by what they are saying, we are all cursed.

Hosea 4:6-7

6. My people are destroyed for lack of knowledge. Because you have rejected knowledge, I also will reject you from being my priest. Since you have forgotten the law of your God, I also will forget your children. 7. The more they multiplied, the more they sinned against me; I will change their glory into shame.

What the Hell?

By religious standards, Hell was the ultimate price to pay for not believing in God or Jesus. Hell, was were Satan lived with all his demons, minions, monsters and the place of eternal torment for non-believers. My siblings and I would sit in church and be told horrendous stories about being burned in Hell's fire for eternity as well as being tormented by demons. We were told that those in hell would be able to look up and see people and loved ones walking around in heaven and beg water from them but no one would hear or help.

As an adult; I know that those stories passed down were to convert non-believers and to control those already converted by using spook-ism. I didn't understand why one would need to be scared into "believing" until I grasped the over-standing that a lot of what I was being taught about hell and faith in general were twisted or outright lies nowhere to be found in the bible. While reading Job, I came across chapter 14 verse 13 and asked myself after reading; why would job ask to be sent to hell to escape his suffering? that was my first thought on how those in the Bible saw it, and how its described to me.

Job 14:13
O that thou wouldest hide me in the Sheol, that thou wouldest keep me secret, until thy wrath be past, that thou wouldest appoint me a set time, and remember me!

Reading this verse lead me to do further research on the word 'Sheol' and what I found was astonishing and eye-opening. The Hebrew word 'Sheol' meant "grave" and not "Hell" as I was told.

Everyone who dies goes to 'Sheol' not just non-believers, but everyone. Pastors, deacons, crack-heads, children, and even you, will go to Sheol. Sheol is not a place of suffering and torment where you could see friends and family members that made it into heaven, walk around in heaven all day. King Solomon stated that God would redeem him from the grave in *Psalms 139:8*. So why would the very wise King Solomon want to "make his bed in Hell" where he would be tormented and burned until God redeemed him? He does state that if he does make his bed in hell that God will be there.

Psalms 139:8
If I ascend up into heaven, thou art there: if I make my bed in hell, behold, thou art there.

In *Genesis 37:35* Israel stated that he would be reunited with his son Joseph in Sheol. So tell me how could all of Israel be saved if the person Israel, himself was being tormented in hell? So as far I could tell 'Sheol' meant grave.

Genesis 37:35
And all his sons and all his daughters rose up to comfort him; but he refused to be comforted; and he said, for I will go down into the grave unto my son mourning. Thus his father wept for him.

As I kept reading I also notice that in regards to the grave, it was not a godless inescapable place as I am made to believe. Also, the Bible never mentions monsters, demons, eternal torment, watching people in heaven in jealousy, reliving how you died in sin every day for the rest of your eternal life or the multitude of other horrible things I was taught.

In *Psalms 49:15* the sons of Korah said that God would redeem them from the grave. That scripture tells me that either their bodies or their souls could leave Hell at some point and was not just for sinners to burn eternally.

Psalms 49:15
But God will redeem my soul from the power of the grave: for he shall receive me. Selah.

And for those of you thinking that the Greek word *'Hades'* means hell, you would be wrong as well. Why then would Hades contain the Elysian Fields and blessed isles in a places hell bent (pun intended) on torturing peoples' souls forever. Hades would then also mean the grave, where everyone went when they died.

The Greek word *Tartarus* is only mentioned once in the entire Bible in *2 Peter 2:4* that means 'Hell' as we think it does. Tartarus or "Hell" is a dark place where the fallen angels are held until God came to judge them.

2 Peter 2:4

For if God spared not the angels that sinned, but cast them down to hell, and delivered them into chains of darkness, to be reserved unto judgment;

Let's also not forget that the same Hell that the fallen angels will enter is the same hell that Satan will be bound up in for one thousand (1000) years before he is released again…. yep I said released again!

So now my rational mind kicks in and ask; why wasn't the torment of hell not given to everyone throughout the Bible that disobeyed God? Or even mentioned as a punishment for not following God's laws and commandments. And by 'everyone' I mean Adam, Cain, Noah, Abraham, lot, the people of Sodom and Gomorrah, Moses, the pharaoh who defied God, Job, Jonah, David, Solomon, Daniel, Ezekiel, Isaiah, or any other Hebrew prophet for that matter.

As per most modern bible scholars, the word "hell" did not appear a single time, in the Hebrew bible, or the Old Testament. Currently the word Hell appears in our modern version of the Bible roughly about 50 times. The appearance of such is widely due to corrupted text and errors in translation, confusing the meaning of the word Sheol for Hell.

The "Authorized" King James Version mentions the word hell 31 times in the Old Testament, and 23 Times in the New Testament. Now in the New King James Version (NKJV) the number of times hell is mentioned has been cut in half with being mentioned 19 times in the Old Testament and 13 times in the New Testament.

TIMES THE WORD "HELL" APPEARS IN THE BIBLE	OT	NT	Total
"Authorized" King James Version (KJV), based on corrupted texts	31	23	54
New King James Version (NKJV), still wrong about Sheol	19	13	32
New International Version (NIV) the best-selling English Bible	0	13	13
American Standard Version (ASV)	0	13	13
New American Standard Bible (NASB)	0	13	13
Holman Christian Standard Bible (HCSB) Southern Baptist	0	11	11
Revised Standard Version (RSV)	0	12	12
New Revised Standard Version (NRSV)	0	12	12
Revised English Bible (REB)	0	13	13
New Living Translation (NLT)	0	13	13
Amplified Bible (AMP)	0	13	13
Darby	0	12	12
New Century Version (NCV)	0	12	12
New American Bible Revised Edition (NABRE) Roman Catholic	0	0	0
Wesley's New Testament (1755)	0	0	0
Scarlett's N.T. (1798)	0	0	0
The New Testament in Greek and English (Kneeland, 1823)	0	0	0
Young's Literal Translation (1891)	0	0	0
Twentieth Century New Testament (1900)	0	0	0
Rotherham's Emphasized Bible (reprinted, 1902)	0	0	0
Fenton's Holy Bible in Modern English (1903)	0	0	0

Weymouth's New Testament in Modern Speech (1903)	0	0	0
Jewish Publication Society Bible Old Testament (1917)	0	0	0
Panin's Numeric English New Testament (1914)	0	0	0
The People's New Covenant (Overbury, 1925)	0	0	0
Hanson's New Covenant (1884)	0	0	0
Western N.T. (1926)	0	0	0
NT of our Lord and Savior Anointed (Tomanek, 1958)	0	0	0
Concordant Literal NT (1983)	0	0	0
The N.T., A Translation (Clementson, 1938)	0	0	0
Emphatic Diaglott, Greek/English Interlinear (Wilson, 1942)	0	0	0
New American Bible (1970)	0	0	0
Restoration of Original Sacred Name Bible (1976)	0	0	0
Tanakh, The Holy Scriptures, Old Testament (1985)	0	0	0
The New Testament, A New Translation (Greber, 1980)	0	0	0
Christian Bible (1991)	0	0	0
World English Bible (in progress)	0	0	0
Orthodox Jewish Brit Chadasha [NT Only]	0	0	0
Original Bible Project (Dr. James Tabor, still in translation)	0	0	0
Zondervan Parallel N.T. in Greek and English (1975)**	0	0	0
Int. NASB-NIV Parallel N.T. in Greek and English (1993)**	0	0	0
A Critical Paraphrase of the N.T. by Vincent T. Roth (1960)	0	0	0

The wages of sin

Romans 6:23
For the wages of sin is death, but the gift of God is eternal life in Christ Jesus our Lord.

When I hear this scripture, I think of, *death in sin*, in two ways. The first thought of death in sin, is the spiritual and the second being the Physical and dying while "not right with God".

I feel that a spiritual death is separation from God. We can all agree that people are going to church faithfully that will die in sin, so I'm not saying that you should go to church to be connected to God or walk around quoting scriptures. However, I'm speaking of operating in kindness and harmony with yourself and those around you. I'm speaking of not doing harm to others and operating from a place of compassion and balance. I feel that the longer you don't connect with God or operate in wickedness or just worldly things, you are removed from the spirit/energy of God and therefor die in sin.

I have felt that disconnect at many points in my life. Some express it as a need to go to church or pray to reconnect to God. We can get so wrapped up our daily living that we only attempt to connect with God or our chosen higher power when we feel a lack and need a blessing (help)
Even if you don't believe in a higher power, or Supreme Being, most of us are walking around spiritually dead (off balance mentally and emotionally) and need balancing.

Physically dying in sin means, for me, that you are not right with God at the point where you pass on and there for not eligible to go to heaven. Not that you are going to hell to be tormented, but there is no "after life" for you, you cease to exist. I will remind you here that growing up in the church I did; we were told that if you called on the name of the lord before you died you could be "saved". And beside that thought of believing that theory would make all the moral teaching obsolete, because all I would need to do after living a life of sin is call on the name of Jesus before I died and I would get into heaven. But what if I died suddenly? What if I didn't see 'it' coming and couldn't call on the name of Jesus and I died in sin? That poses a problem for the previous theory, right? That would mean that I can better serve myself by living by the laws and commandments that God set for me and assure my place in heaven so I could return and rule the earth with the other saints.

When thinking of spirituality and religion and asked myself the question; why would God give man free-will and then punish him/her for not choosing the 'right' path?

That question led me to think that; in the bible, the angles had to do God's will, and man was given free will at a point, so how could Satan, once an angel of heaven who had no free will; turn against God and become his archenemy. In the Qur'an, the angels had to do God will, but man and the jinn had free will. Per the **Qur'an**, one of the Jinn abused his free-will in front of God by refusing to bow down to Adam when God ordered angels and **jinn** to do so. For disobeying God, he was expelled from Heaven and called "Shaytān" (Satan).

Now in the Tanakh (old testament) there is nothing about angles rebelling against God, no one named the devil, no one named Lucifer, and no place known as hell. Furthermore, in the Jewish Tanakh, which is older than the Christian bible, the one people refer to as the devil, was called the "Ha-Satan", which means "the Tempter". The "Ha-Satan" was an angel of God, given the task by God to tempt the Jews from reading the Torah and to test their faith. That makes him an employee of God, not a fallen angel, nor a rebellious angel seeking the thrown of heaven. how else would the "tempter", Ha-Satan, be allowed to tempt Jesus in **Matthew 4: 1-11**

Matthew 4: 1-11
4 Then Jesus was led by the Spirit into the wilderness to be tempted[a] by the devil.
2 After fasting forty days and forty nights, he was hungry.
3 The tempter came to him and said, "If you are the Son of God, tell these stones to become bread."
4 Jesus answered, "It is written: 'Man shall not live on bread alone, but on every word that comes from the mouth of God.'[b]"
5 Then the devil took him to the holy city and had him stand on the highest point of the temple.
6 "If you are the Son of God," he said, "throw yourself down. For it is written:
"'He will command his angels concerning you,
   and they will lift you up in their hands,
   so that you will not strike your foot against a stone.'[c]"
7 Jesus answered him, "It is also written: 'Do not put the Lord your God to the test.'[d]"

8 Again, the devil took him to a very high mountain and showed him all the kingdoms of the world and their splendor.
9 "All this I will give you," he said, "if you will bow down and worship me."
10 Jesus said to him, "Away from me, Satan! For it is written: 'Worship the Lord your God, and serve him only.'[e]"
11 Then the devil left him, and angels came and attended him.

I believe in the universal law that you have the right to choose your path but you also must take with it the consequences of your choice. All too often we hide behind religion and scripture to harm people thinking our beliefs or faith will absolve us from the consequences of our actions. Whether you believe in Hell or not, what you do will ultimately end up coming back to you.

Witchcraft in the church

1. Does your church teach that God only speaks, or must speak to them first before speaking with you?

Too often we forget that the individuals leading the church are regular flawed human beings just like us. We cast this divine presence onto church leadership because they may know more about religion than us or can quote scripture from memory. We may revere them because they look good, dress nice, and seem to have it all together as though God has shown them favor. That's very unfortunate that we do that, as it's also unfair for leadership to take advantage of their positions.

Often we find that church figure heads from the pastor down to junior deacons attempt to sway the views, opinions and actions of the church body by stating or giving the impression that they have a more divine connection to God and Gods will than the average church goer. We've all been told, on one occasion or another, the phrase, *"God told me to tell you"* or *"God placed on my heart to let you know"* followed by some statement from a church member, leadership or even a family member.

As I stated in an earlier chapter, I believe that God will tell you what he has to and through someone or something send confirmation of that thing. It's this very reason why I am weary of people and their claim to have some insight on what I need to be doing with my life. Those "God sent" messages are usually their will for us and not the will of God they are trying to convey. It's a passive aggressive tactic used by individuals who are afraid that their message is too harsh for you, or that you just simply won't handle what they must say to you well so they use "God told me" as an irrefutable vessel.

Even when the statement is followed by a message of praise or encouragement, it's still someone attempting to claim God is using them as a messenger.

Leviticus 19:31
Do not turn to mediums or spiritist; do not seek them out to be defiled by them.

Leviticus 20:6
I will set my face against anyone who turns to mediums and spiritists to prostitute themselves by following them, and I will cut them off from their people.

Deuteronomy 18:10-12
10 "There shall not be found among you anyone who makes his son or his daughter pass through the fire, one who uses divination, one who practices witchcraft, or one who interprets omens, or a sorcerer, 11 or one who casts a spell, or a medium, or a spiritist, or one who calls up the dead. 12 "For whoever does these things is detestable to

the LORD; and because of these detestable things the LORD your God will drive them out before you....

2. Are you forbidden to talk to anyone that has left the church?

The church should not operate like a street gang. People should be allowed to leave if they feel that church is not serving their spiritual needs. The church could be too far or life circumstances could lead someone to change places of worship.

Being excommunicated from a church and its members is a control tactic used by cult leaders, not church leaders. It's a way of keeping that disgruntled member from reaching the rest of the church body and pulling them away as well.

I've witnessed a church leader instruct his congregation to avoid personal fellowship with any former member of that church. He did not want those rebellious sheep to lead any of his flock astray. So, if your parents, siblings, best friends or any friend no longer attended that church, you were not to communicate with them at all and sever all ties.

I've also witnessed a pastor refusing a family's wish to perform burial services at the church because the woman was no longer a member of his church. Even though she was a member of the church for over 30 plus years, and her relatives were still current members; she was denied services all because she stopped being an active member of the church due to failing health.

3. Does your church (over-emphasize) the teaching of submission to church leadership?

If the message of being obedient to church leadership is drilled into your head week after week, it will eventually become your way of thinking. Generally, *Ephesians 6:5* is read to the church to remind the congregation that they need to be obedient to their pastor.

Ephesians 6:5
Servants, be obedient to them that are your masters according to the flesh, with fear and trembling, in singleness of your heart, as unto Christ

If we continue to read the entire passage like we are supposed to, we find greater clarity and a charge to master and servant, leadership and flock.

Ephesians 6:6-9
6 Not with eye service, as men pleasers; but as the servants of Christ, doing the will of God from the heart;
7 With good will doing service, as to the Lord, and not to men:

8 Knowing that whatsoever good thing any man doeth, the same shall he receives of the Lord, whether he be bond or free.

9 And, ye masters, do the same things unto them, forbearing threatening: knowing that your master also is in heaven; neither is there respect of persons with him.

We are charge with doing the will of God, not man! This is where some church leadership needs you to believe that they know the will of God over your life better than you do.

4. Are you forbidden to visit any church outside of your denomination or fellowship?

Are the doctrines so different that it would poison your faith to visit another church? Is there a fight for membership that your pastor fears losing you to another church/pastor?

It's more about fear that you will travel outside the scope of their influence and awaken from the spell/brainwashing over you. It's the fear that someone will teach you another way or the truth. There is no reason a church or pastor should hinder you from visiting another church or another denomination.

It should not be the concern of anyone about which other church you visit. There is no law or commandment written that forbids attending another church or church of another denomination.

5. Are relationships/marriages broken by church leadership?

The act of interfering in relationships goes beyond the realm of church members or leadership interjecting in an unhealthy relationship and pleading for you to seek help or counseling. I'm sure we all have stories about the pastor fathering other illegitimate children outside of his marriage, or church leaders taking advantage of women in the church. I recount an incident in the church I grew up in, where the pastor fathered a child outside of his marriage and attempted to get his son to marry his mistress and claim the child.

Churches should not be interfering with your relationship(s) or marriage outside of giving sound unbiased advice if you are seeking it. I've also witnessed in the church a pastor telling a young woman that her current boyfriend (who wasn't a church member) wasn't right for her and that her true GOD given boyfriend was there in the church [of course, a current member of the church].

6. Are people manipulated into giving and/or taken advantage of financially?

Being manipulated is covered in detail in previous essays in this book. However, the message is clear, selling prayer cloths, holy oil, or made to feel guilty into giving financially; it is wrong and not of GOD.

When that collection plate passed more than once, because "the church" is short of its financial goal, it's not of GOD. You are no longer giving out of the kindness of your heart but paying a bill.

7. Do all decisions in your personal life have to be approved by leadership?

If you are required to seek council from church leadership to get their approval on matters of your personal life, then you are seriously going down the wrong path. You are no longer seeking GOD for assistance, but man. GOD can speak to you directly and never needed an interpreter. Its Gods will be done, not your pastors or deacons.

It's an arrogant mindset to feel that you need to control people's lives away from the church. How can a man manage the affairs of himself, his own family, and multiple church members? There's one thing to seek counsel on a matter, but to get approval for decisions you make for yourself and/or family is something altogether different.

8. Are you forbidden to fellowship with your family if they are not saved or belong to your church?

Isolation is a form of isolating you from outside influences. You are being taught that the church family is more important than your own family, and in my opinion, at this point, your church family becomes a cult. In the example of Yeshua (Jesus), He did not say only go to "saved" people or just converse with people in the church. It's okay to want to have all *saved* friends, but to

willfully only interact with people of your church just seems bizarre to me.

9. Does leadership teach that their church is the only true church?

That claim is rooted in control. If you should ever witness anyone making this claim, leave immediately. Knowing that Christianity was derived from another religion, Judaism, and intermingled with paganism would be a clear indication that a claim such as that is false.

10. Does leadership curse anyone that leaves the church?

If church leadership warns against leaving their church with tales of horror and doom as mine did, leave immediately. Too many times, church leadership will advise not to go from under their divine protection or some other nonsense to keep their membership numbers high. They trick you into believing that you are only blessed if you are tied to them somehow.

I was told the same story on occasion about the man my pastor warned not to leave and who was met with death soon after. The pastor of the church I grew up in even refused to perform funeral services for a member who spent the better part of her life on the pews in his church. She left due to old age because getting back and forth was tiresome but then was considered a non-member once she stopped

attending. The fact that the woman was blood-related to him made matters worse.

11. Are people publicly embarrassed or humiliated by leadership?

A tactic such as public humiliation is used to invoke fear in its membership. If you're being publicly embarrassed or humiliated for whatever the reason; it's wrong. There is no reason you should be made an example of in this manner to the church body. If you're being made an example of because you disobeyed the church leadership or fell short of some ungodly metric the church is holding you to, it's time to consider going somewhere else. Where is the compassion, understanding and love?

The Christmas Lie

Christmas is one of the most celebrated religious holidays around the world. It's supposed to represent the birth of Christ, the savior, being born to the world. The holiday ushers in the spirit of hope, the mood of giving, forgiving, and making amends.

unfortunately, i could never get complete answers to the questions regarding the holiday. The answers I was given never made sense to me. As the story goes, Yeshua (Jesus) was born in a manger. the star represented the North Star that the three kings followed to find Yeshua (Jesus). When it came to explaining the tree and the virgin birth, I was dismissed. Once I began reading, researching, and learning for myself, I quickly learned that the holiday of Christmas is not even in the Bible, but all the elements that the holiday is made of are.

I came across some information in the Bible, Jeremiah 10:2-4, that sounded strikingly like a Christmas tree and God's people being warned not to take part.

Jeremiah 10:2-4

"Learn not the way of the heathen, and be not dismayed at the signs of heaven; (astrology) for the heathen are dismayed at them...For the customs of the people are vain: for one cuts a tree out of the forest, the work of the hands of the workman, with the axe. They deck it with silver and with gold; they fasten it with nails and with hammers that it move not."

That sounds like a description of a Christmas tree if I ever heard one.

That wasn't enough for me, I had to understand why the Most-High didn't want his people taking part in such a thing so I took to the bible and read about Babylon.

Now enters the knowledge I learned from reading about King Nimrod, also known as the Ba'al the 'Sun-god', the king of Babylon. I will give you the summarized version of what I learned because the story can be lengthy. Nimrod married his mother, Semiramis, the son of Jacob, Esau, killed Nimrod after Shem, the son of Noah, put a bounty on his head. After Nimrods death, his wife/mother deified him and he became Ba'al [which means, lord or husband]. when she told the Babylonians that Nimrod was being reincarnated in her belly after he impregnated her with his sun-rays and will reincarnate himself as her new son Tammuz. [Ezekiel 8:14]

Ezekiel 8:14,15

14 Then He brought me to the entrance of the gate of the LORD's house which was toward the north; and behold, women were sitting there weeping for Tammuz. 15 He said to me, "Do you see this, son of man? Yet you will see still greater abominations than these."

During all of this she also came up with a plan to stay the queen of Babylon. Semiramis said that a dead tree trunk turned into a tall evergreen tree overnight which was to represent new life for her dead husband/son. Semiramis also told them that every year Nimrod dies on December 21th [which is the winter solstice, shortest day of the year] and is reborn as the Ba'al, the 'sun-God' on December 25th, Nimrod returns to the forest and leaves gifts under the tree. Is the starting to sound familiar yet?

Every year on Tammuz birthday, Babylonians are instructed to go to the forest and leave gifts under a tree to honor Nimrod. The tree has its significance because it's said that Nimrod was 'cut down' like a tree. Furthermore, the Babylonians were told to go cut down a evergreen tree, like the one that magically appeared over night after Nimrods' death, and take it home and decorate it with silver and gold balls which were to represent Nimrods testicles.

Now Nimrod's testicles come into play because per Babylonian history, when Nimrod was killed his body was chopped up and sent to different parts of Babylon to warn people not to sacrifice babies to Moloch [ancient pagan God that required child sacrifice

– God warns of this in the Bible as well] the only body part that was ever found of Nimrod was his penis. His wife decided to erect [no pun intended] a giant image of his penis, called an obelisk.

Obelisk

1. A stone pillar, typically having a square or rectangular cross section and a pyramidal top, set up as a monument or landmark.

synonyms: pillar, column, needle, shaft, monolith, monument

I need to mention here; better yet remind you that we are instructed several places in the Bible not to worship idols and to destroy those types of structures which still appear on most churches today.

Deuteronomy 7:4-6

For they will turn your sons away from following me to serve other gods; then the anger of the LORD will be kindled against you and He will quickly destroy you. 5 "But thus you shall do to them: you shall tear down their altars, and smash their sacred pillars, and hew down their Asherim, and burn their graven images with fire. 6 "For you are a holy people to the LORD your God; the LORD your God has chosen you to be a people for His own possession out of all the peoples who are on the face of the earth.

Deuteronomy 12:2-4

2 "You shall utterly destroy all the places where the nations whom you shall dispossess serve their gods, on the high mountain and on the hills and under every green tree. 3 "You shall tear down their altars and smash their sacred pillars and burn their Asherim with fire and you shall cut down the engraved images of their gods and obliterate their name from that place. 4 "You shall not act like this toward the LORD you God.

Jeremiah 43:12, 13

12 "And I shall set fire to the temples of the gods of Egypt, and he will burn them and take them captive. So, he will wrap himself with the land of Egypt as a shepherd wraps himself with his garment, and he will depart from there safely. 13 He will also shatter the obelisks of Heliopolis, which is in the land of Egypt; and the temples of the gods of Egypt he will burn with fire.

Hosea 10:1-3

1. Israel is a luxuriant vine; He produces fruit for himself. The more his fruit, the more altars he made; the richer his land, the better he made the sacred pillars. 2 Their heart is faithless; now they must bear their guilt. The LORD will break down their altars and destroy their sacred pillars *3.*

Surely now they will say, "We have no king, for we do not revere the LORD. As for the king, what can he do for us?"…

Exodus 34:12-14

12"Watch yourself that you make no covenant with the inhabitants of the land into which you are going, or it will become a snare in your midst. **"But rather, you are to tear down their altars and smash their sacred pillars and cut down their Asherim. 14 for you shall not worship any other god, for the LORD, whose name is jealous, is a jealous God.**

Exodus 23:24

24 "You shall not worship their gods, nor serve them, nor do according to their deeds; but you shall utterly overthrow them and break their sacred pillars in pieces.

Note: *Asherah/Asherim*: groves (sacred trees for idol worship); *associated with Babylonian* (Astarte/Ishtar) – Canaanite religion

Now we can clearly see that the 'Christmas tree" is an Asherah pole for honoring Tammuz aka the sun-god and the ornaments are supposed to represent Nimrod's testicles. How again is this supposed to be a representation of the birth of Christ? Sadly, we cling to the ignorance of our parents, who just did what they were told or just followed what was deemed normal, and our grand and great-grandparents who were given false information or made to submit to these holidays and celebrations which are an abomination before God.

I find when you explain this to people, and they see the truth for themselves, they dismiss this information. Which, in large part, right in the same bible that collects dust on their nightstand and bookshelves at home, or they quickly say the celebration is mainly for the kids, so why does it matter. And if you are one of those who believe that excuse, you are part of the problem and are still not following what the Most-High instructed you to do.

Terrorist in America

For at least the last decade, we have been inundated with newscasts, headlines, images, and propaganda about radical Islam and the terror network hell-bent on killing Americans and destroying this country.

I normally try to hold my tongue when I hear someone regurgitating messages of hate towards anyone and or anybody. In a recent argument with a close friend of mine, who is an ordained pastor in the Christian faith, I asked him a question that I could not get a straight answer too. I asked him, What about the war on radical Christians?? His head turned slightly to the side and mouth parted opened; he stood silent for a few seconds and asked what I was talking about when he could finally speak. I told him, in my opinion, there should also be a war on radical Christians as well because more problems arise from radical Christians than any other American group I could readily think of. I had to remind him that the Klu Klux Klan is a Christian group, and as well as the Christian crusades from 1095 to 1291, the entire world can read about in the bible and in history books.

I asked him, what makes Christian's reasons for war different from any other religion, that they are singled out? He began to spew passages and verses from the bible about how it was God's plan to spread his message all over the land (which is not in the bible I may add), then I told him I wanted his opinion, not an auto-response from the bible. I wanted to know if anywhere in the time he studied in theology school was a mention ever made about the reasons Christian churches never openly discuss the documented wars started in the name of spreading the

Word of Jesus Christ or taking/"reclaiming" land. why would Jesus, who brings a message of love and redemption, have his message delivered by those who chose to kill and destroy? (Which directly contradicts, "Thou shall not kill")

During the conversation, I presented such evidence like the colonial conquest where Native Americans in North, South, and Central America where slaughtered over several generations to the tune of 20 million. Or in Bosnia, where the genocide of over three hundred thousand Muslims took place along with a systematic rape of Muslim women by Christian Serbians from 1992 to 1995. We also spoke about the situation in Rwanda back in 1994, where over nine hundred thousand Rwandans were also slaughtered amid a population that is over ninety percent, Christian. We can even fast forward this conversation to the present day where nuns sit outside of the abortion clinics handing out brochures with pictures of dismembered babies and screaming of impending doom on women's souls if they terminate a child. Or the clear majority of groups that rise amid issue where Christians feel the laws of the bible are being broken, and use violent means to get their point across. I want to take the time to interject that there is a clear divide between the laws in the bible and religious, moral doctrine.

The last question I asked the reverend was, why does the Qur'an mention Jesus, but the bible does not say Muhammad? Churchgoers will tell you their version of how the Islamic faith came about by quoting genesis chapters 16 through 18 etc. but the Qur'an mentions that Jesus was a profit of the Most-High God. Again in my opinion those radical Christians seem more like bullies, today and throughout history. But then again most people who are fanatics or radical in their beliefs of anything tend to take things to far, that's Muslim, Christian, Buddhist, sports fans etc. It's like when someone first find religion they go full force quoting passages and trying to convert anyone who will listen. And again, there will always be those few that will have a different understanding and attempt to pervert something for their purposes.

Now before you begin to believe I'm anti-Christian or anti-religion, I'm not. I'm just a man who sees the contradiction in the way things are. When it comes down to who the offending party is. I'm pinpointing an issue with religious wars or fighting for what's "seemingly" right when the history of this nation is filled with evil deeds from a peaceful religion. I haven't even begun to talk about the long-term effect of the doctrines and stipulation churches put on parishioners that tend to act a lot like mind control and may I add, cannot be found in any bible. My feelings are, a religion that doesn't acknowledge the validity of any other religion by stating it's the only way into heaven, and everyone else will burn in hell, seems wrong and severely closed-minded to me. If God created the heaven and the earth and all that is in it, who are you to say who's going to heaven and who isn't.

One again, I'm a very spiritual and believe in God. But Before I graduated from religion, I was raised as a "non-denominational Christian" which is a denomination, better known as the church of God in Christ (C.O.G.I.C) and to this day I read the bible, as well as the Qur'an, Torah etc., go to church and all out have a personal relationship with God. It's just that now I don't do religion at all but anyway you get my point.

references:

I. the first, 1095-1099, called by Pope Urban II and led by Peter the Hermit, Walter the Penniless, Godfrey of Bouillon, Baldwin and Eustace of Flanders, and others (see also first crusade);

II. the second, 1147-49, headed by King Louis VII who was enlisted by Bernard of Clairvaux, was a disastrous failure, including the loss of one of the four Latin Kingdoms, the Duchy of Edessa;

III. the third, 1188-92, proclaimed by Pope Gregory VIII in the wake of the catastrophe of the second crusade, which conducted by Emperor Frederick Barbarossa, King Philip Augustus of France and King Richard "Coeur-de-Lion" of England;

IV. the fourth, during which Constantinople was sacked, 1202-1204 (see also fourth crusade);

V. the fifth, which included the conquest of Damietta, 1217-1221;

VI. the sixth, in which Frederick II took part (1228-29); also Thibaud de Champagne and Richard of Cornwall (1239);

VII. the seventh, led by St. Louis (Louis IX of France), 1248-50;

How you pray

Let's agree right now to stop with the fancy prayers. I know there are "prayer warriors" and people who can pray the devil out of people and blah blah blah but let's get to the root of it all. We know prayer is how we offer supplication to God and give thanks for grace and mercy extended to us, or for most people; put in our request to our heavenly father like he was some magic genie here to grant our every wish. I'm sure by now you can tell at this point that I'm about to tell you where you have gone in this manner.

In **James 5:16** it states that the effectual fervent prayer availeth much. **Effectual** means; successful in producing a desired or intended result; effective. And **Fervent** means; having or displaying a passionate intensity. **Availeth/avail** means; use or take advantage of something.

What this means to me is that if you are successful in giving a passionately intense (sincere) prayer, that prayer will give you an advantage in whatever you desire. It also was written as an earnest, and sincere prayer avails much. **Earnest** means; resulting from or showing sincere and intense conviction and **sincere** means, free from pretense or deceit; proceeding from genuine feelings. So an intense, genuine prayer free from deceit gives you an advantage.

James 5:15 - 17

*15 **And the prayer of faith shall save the sick, and the Lord shall raise him up; and if he have committed sins, they shall be forgiven him.***

[16] Confess your faults one to another, and pray one for another, that ye may be healed. The effectual fervent prayer of a righteous man availeth much. [17] Elias was a man subject to like passions as we are, and he prayed earnestly that it might not rain: and it rained not on the earth by the space of three years and six months.

So who started the trend of 'posturing' with these prayers at church? We've all sat through the long benediction prayers during Sunday service. Or we can think of the one person we hate to have pray because he or she takes so long. These lengthy prayers are often far from sincere and full of arrogance. And it's not necessarily the praying aloud; that's the issue. But most often, when people pray aloud, they are seldom sincere and are just putting on a show. In **_Matthew 6:5_**, Jesus says, don't be like the hypocrites, because they love to pray in the open to be seen by people. Again, Jesus is not condemning the fact that people prayed out loud, but that they were putting on a public show for their ego or personal gain.

Matthew 6:5

"And when you pray, do not be like the hypocrites, for they love to pray standing in the synagogues and on the street corners to be seen by men. I tell you the truth, they have received their reward in full."

Too often we attempt to "wow" our audience as we pray, with long winded rants that go on for forever. And yes its wrong, but the greater sin is praying with arrogance. In **_Luke 18:10-14_**, Jesus gives a parable about two men; one a Pharisee and the other a tax collector.

The Pharisee stood by himself and prayed like most of us pray today, with some self-righteous prayer, giving little thanks and asking for a great deal.
But the tax collector stood at a distance. Humble in his spirit and offers an earnest and sincere prayer before God. And at the end of the parable Jesus said "I tell you that this man, rather than the other, went home justified before God. Jesus goes on to state that every person that exalt themselves will be humbled, and those who humble themselves will be exalted.

Luke 18:10-14

"Two men went up into the temple to pray, one a Pharisee and the other a tax collector. The Pharisee, standing by himself, prayed thus: 'God, I thank you that I am not like other men, extortioners, unjust, adulterers, or even like this tax collector. I fast twice a week; I give tithes of all that I get.' But the tax collector, standing far off, would not even lift up his eyes to heaven, but beat his breast, saying, 'God, be merciful to me, a sinner!' I tell you, this man went down to his house justified, rather than the other. For everyone who exalts himself will be humbled, but the one who humbles himself will be exalted."

Now notice that the tax collector prayed aloud, but his prayer was from a humble heart, and God accepted it. The sin of the Pharisees was not that he gave a public prayer, but the prayer is filled with arrogance. If you read *Luke 20:46-47*, you can see that Jesus condemns the hypocrisy of pretending to have a relationship with God while oppressing the very people God loves. You can change the word "oppressing" to "taking advantage" of the very people he loves, like so many of the people in the church, including leadership.

Luke 20:46-47

"Beware of the scribes, who like to walk around in long robes, and love greetings in the marketplaces and the best seats in the synagogues and the places of honor at feasts, who devour widows' houses and for a pretense make long prayers. They will receive the greater condemnation"

How often do we offer prayer without making a request? Do you thank God for the things you already have or the current situation?

It appears the only time we can offer God an earnest and sincere prayer is when we are hurting mentally, spiritually, or emotionally. We come to God with our heads bowed, tears running down our face, and hands extended wanting God to hear and answer our prayers. Whether we pray for ourselves or others, it's the prayers of the righteous that get through.

The concept that only the prayers of the righteous get heard is surprisingly foreign to 99% of believers. We know that you could offer up prayer at any time and any place. I stopped allowing people to pray for me and stopped asking when I came into the knowledge that not everyone is in the right mindset or spirit to pray for me. I don't know if you and God are on good terms, and I am a man of a mature spiritual age and knowledgeable enough to pray for myself. **Proverbs 15:29** says that only the righteous get their prayers heard, which is disheartening because I don't know any honest people, including myself.

Proverbs 15:29

"The LORD is far from the wicked but he hears the prayer of the righteous."

In *Ephesians 5:20*, Paul tells the church to "give thanks always and for everything to God the Father in the name of our Lord Jesus Christ." Praying aloud is one-way churchgoers worship God and encourage one another. The thing is that Jesus condemns the arrogance and hypocrisy in prayer. For someone who is not right with God to lead a public prayer as though he or she had much to brag about is the kind of hypocrisy that Jesus didn't like. To use public prayer to showboat or to impress others is wrong. We know a sincere prayer from a humble heart is always welcome by God and can be an encouragement to those who hear it.

Matthew 6:1-34

"Beware of practicing your righteousness before other people in order to be seen by them, for then you will have no reward from your Father who is in heaven. "Thus, when you give to the needy, sound no trumpet before you, as the hypocrites do in the synagogues and in the streets, that they may be praised by others. Truly, I say to you, they have received their reward. But

when you give to the needy, do not let your left hand know what your right hand is doing, so that your giving may be in secret. And your Father who sees in secret will reward you. "And when you pray, you must not be like the hypocrites. For they love to stand and pray in the synagogues and at the street corners, that they may be seen by others. Truly, I say to you, they have received their reward.

The Lord's Prayer

This idea of the famous prayer may come as a surprise to most, but "The lord's prayer" is an example, not an actual prayer. The Lord's Prayer appears in two places in the Bible. In the book of Luke, **Luke 11:2-4**, Jesus was praying, by himself, and when he finished, one of his disciples asked him, "Lord, teach us how to pray the way John taught his disciples," referring to John the Baptist. Jesus responded, "When you pray, say," and at that point, he gave the disciples the example of what we know as the Lord's Prayer

But in the book of Matthew, **Matthew 6:9-13** toward the end of the Sermon on the Mount, Jesus warns the disciples against praying with long, empty phrases and many words. "Do not be like them," he says, "for your Father knows what you need before you ask him. Pray then in this way..." he then gives the Lord's Prayer.

Matthew 6:9-13 (KJV)
9 After this manner therefore pray ye: Our Father which art in heaven, Hallowed be thy name.
10 Thy kingdom come, Thy will be done in earth, as it is in heaven.
11 Give us this day our daily bread.
12 And forgive us our debts, as we forgive our debtors.

**¹³ *And lead us not into temptation, but deliver us from evil:
For thine is the kingdom, and the power, and the glory,
forever. Amen.***

We can split hairs over the *"When you pray, say"* and *"Pray
then in this way."* But if Jesus spoke against long-winded
prayers and "the lord's prayer" is the only prayer to be said,
would we ever get any of our prayers answered? Or would
you be comfortable with not praying because God knows
what you want before you ask him? Would you be able to
accept God's will for your life? Think about that.

Covered or Uncovered

This subtopic is uniquely funny to me. I would use this very
topic to piss off the uninformed whenever i could. I often
tell the story of me walking into a church and immediately
being address and asked to remove my hat. I would quickly
ask the requester why I should remove my cap. I have, to
date, never gotten a biblical answer as to why I should not
walk into church with a hat beside the reason for respect for
being in the 'House of the lord' which I should treat like any
other house in which I should show respect and remove my
covering.

A later example, as I recall being in a church meeting, and a
benediction prayer started before we departed the meeting.
Everyone stood and removed their hat and bowed their
head for prayer. When the gentleman that was praying
notice that I didn't remove my cap, he requested that I

remove mine. And when I asked why he stated that because you are supposed to remove your cap while praying. (This is the point where I chose to educate him) I asked him who was leading the communal prayer; he identified himself as the one that would lead the prayer. I then asked (for clarities sake) was I and everyone in the room to pray a separate prayer or listen to the prayer he was leading. He then stated that he was leading the prayer and that we were to listen to him. I quickly pointed him to

1 Corinthians 11:2-16 and informed him that the individual who is offering up the prayer must remove his hat/covering. As usual, before the gentleman even cracked open a bible to confirm, I was informed that I was wrong. But scripture vindicated me, and another believer was educated, not without a fight, however.

1 Corinthians 11:2-16

Now I commend you because you remember me in everything and maintain the traditions even as I delivered them to you. But I want you to understand that the head of every man is Christ, the head of a wife is her husband, and the head of Christ is God. Every man who prays or prophesies with his head covered dishonors his head, but every wife who prays or prophesies with her head uncovered dishonors her head, since it is the same as if her head were shaven. For if a wife will not cover her head, then she should cut her hair short. But since it is disgraceful for a wife to cut off her hair or shave her head, let her cover her head

If you are the type of person to say your prayer privately, while another person is saying one aloud, then, by all means, remove your covering and follow what Paul stated. If you agree that men, in general, should remove their hats when entering a building...any building, then cool, remove your covering. And trust me, I'm not saying you go and be rebellious, I want you to Over-stand what it means to keep or remove your cover.

Where is Heaven?

From what I hear, Heaven may be in the Bermuda triangle. Or possibly Heaven is in the clouds just beyond our eyesight. Others believe that Heaven may be deep within the earth's crust, were multiple alien races crash-landed and still reside today. These aliens have periodically come to the earth's surface to impart knowledge and wisdom [this is an actual theory] about science and technology for centuries.

I won't go too far down that rabbit hole on this one, I will stick to the confines of the perception of Heaven in the Bible. My first impression of Heaven was that it is beautiful beyond imagination; there is mansion everywhere, warm weather every day, the streets are paved with gold, angels floating or flying around, and we would be in constant worship of God. Heaven is where we would reunite with relatives and friends who've passed on before we did and live happily ever after.

Why wouldn't anyone strive to get to Heaven? No more pain, suffering or trouble; a place where we could finally be free of stress and worry. But the thought of living in Heaven forever and ever is not found in the Bible at all. While reading the Bible, for myself, I found that in **Revelation 20**; God will purge evil from the earth for about one thousand (1000) years, before he re-releases Satan. So, for that thousands of years, the saints will be in Heaven, and the wicked will be in the ground, not hell, but Sheol (the grave). I believe this is called the first resurrection. During this time, God is creating a new heaven and a new earth. If we were to spend eternity in Heaven, why would God create new earth?

In *Isaiah 65:17,* it states that God has created a new heaven and a new earth where the saint would reside.

Revelations 20

Then I saw an angel coming down from heaven, having the key to the bottomless pit and a great chain in his hand. ² He laid hold of the dragon, that serpent of old, who is the Devil and Satan, and bound him for a thousand years; ³ and he cast him into the bottomless pit, and shut him up, and set a seal on him, so that he should deceive the nations no more till the thousand years were finished. But after these things he must be released for a little while.

Isaiah 65:17

"For behold, I create new heavens and a new earth, and the former things shall not be remembered or come into mind.

I want to note here that the Bible mentions two resurrections. The first at the beginning of the thousand years and the second at the end of those thousand years. During the first resurrection, all of God's children will come back to life and be with Jesus. That's when the thousand years of peace is to begin; this is called the resurrection of the righteous. The Bible I have doesn't make mention of the "being/reigning," meaning with Jesus is on earth or in heaven, so that may still be up for debate. But what's not debatable is that no matter where we reside during the first resurrection, it's only for a thousand years.

Isaiah 26:19

Your dead shall live; their bodies shall rise.
You who dwell in the dust, awake and sing for joy!
For your dew is a dew of light, and the earth will give
birth to the dead.

Revelations 20:4

And I saw thrones, and they sat on them, and judgment was committed to them. Then I saw the souls of those who had been beheaded for their witness to Jesus and for the word of God, who had not worshiped the beast or his image, and had not received his mark on their foreheads or on their hands. And they lived and reigned with Christ for a thousand years. ⁵ But the rest of the dead did not live again until the thousand years were finished. This is the first resurrection. ⁶ Blessed and holy is he who has part in the first resurrection. Over such the second death has no power, but they shall be priests of God and of Christ, and shall reign with Him a thousand years.

Once the thousand years are up, the second resurrection will take place. This resurrection is called the resurrection of damnation or the resurrection of the damned. And by comparing scripture, two things seem to take place. The spirits of the righteous rejoin their bodies, and the wicked called out the grave. Rejoining their bodies is a logical explanation for saints resurrected after the 1000 years. And I'll assume that the wicked are called out the grave in spirit for judgment.

John 5:28-29

28 Do not marvel at this; for the hour is coming in which all who are in the graves will hear His voice 29 and come forth—those who have done good, to the resurrection of life, and those who have done evil, to the resurrection of condemnation

During the thousand years of peace, the righteous are in Heaven with God. And possibly some still in the grave [maybe]? The wicked are just among the earth or in the grave, and perhaps some still living? I didn't find clarity in the Bible on that matter, so yes, I'm just as confused as you are. But the Bible states that they are neither buried or living and a few other things. The essential things are that those still left here are never given a chance to repent.

In the rapture stories my mother, and the church, used to scare us with, would mention that during this time, there would be monsters and demons torturing those "left behind" until Jesus return to pass judgment on the world. And as far as we can tell, by reading the Bible, that's not the case.

Who created these horrendous stories? There is a description in the Bible about how the new Heaven would look. But no description of Hell or monsters at all, but we here story after story and account after account of how both places look.

Questions

The Following are questions I've gathered from my own journey to knowing God for myself as well, speaking with individuals, I feel every believer can ask themselves to begin their own spiritual journey.

Question:

Can I trust my holy book?

Answer: [Yes/No – Why/Why Not]

Question:

Who is God to me?

Answer:

Question:

What makes my religion different than any other religion?

Answer:

Question:

Is my faith being used to serve another's agenda?

Answer:

Question:

Is the God I serve the God of my ancestors?

Answer: Answer: [Yes/No – Why/Why Not]

Question:

How has by religion/Faith been influenced?

Answer: [Yes/No – Why/Why Not – By Whom]

Question:

Do I have a genuine connection with God?

Answer: [Yes/No – Why/Why Not]

Question:

Do I know the Holy book for myself?

Answer: [Yes/No – Why/Why Not]

The following is a list of quotes that are widely used but are not actually listed in the Bible. If the quote is found in the Bible, it's grossly misquoted.

1. Moderation in all things.
2. Once saved, always saved.
3. Better to cast your seed....
4. Spare the rod, spoil the child.
5. To thine own self be true.
6. Do unto others as you would have them do unto you.
7. God helps those who help themselves.
8. Money is the root of all evil.
9. Cleanliness is next to godliness.
10. This too shall pass.
11. The eye is the window to the soul.
12. God works in mysterious ways.
13. The lion shall lay down with the lamb.
14. Pride comes before the fall.

Other things not found in the bible:

1. The Three Wise men
2. The Sinner's Prayer
3. Wedding Vows
4. The Seven Deadly Sins
5. The Trinity

Connect with Faraji Toure'

www.facebook.com/farajitoure

www.twitter.com/iamfarajitoure

www.instagram.com/iamfarajitoure

Farajitoure@gmail.com

About the Author

ABOUT FARAJI TOURE'

Faraji is a Swahili word that means consolation; to console or to heal, and as a strategist, consultant, speaker, radio personality and community builder, it is my purpose to work with professionals, entrepreneurs, aspiring authors and individuals to help them pursue work or to work in an area that they are passionate about, create lives that make the world a better place, and to console and heal those dealing with brokenness in their lives by strategically helping them to navigate through life. This is done through personal coaching, business consulting, co-authorships, speaking engagements and living my unapologetic truth, every day of my life.

<u>NOTES:</u>

NOTES:

NOTES: